AN EVANGELIZING
CATECHESIS

AN EVANGELIZING CATECHESIS

Teaching from Your Encounter with Christ

James C. Pauley

Nihil Obstat
Msgr. Michael Heintz, Ph.D.
Censor Librorum

Imprimatur
✠ Kevin C. Rhoades
Bishop of Fort Wayne-South Bend
April 9, 2020

The Nihil Obstat and Imprimatur are official declarations that a book is free from doctrinal or moral error. It is not implied that those who have granted the Nihil Obstat and Imprimatur agree with the contents, opinions, or statements expressed.

Except where noted, the Scripture citations used in this work are taken from the *New American Bible*, revised edition © 2010, 1991, 1970 Confraternity of Christian Doctrine, Washington, DC, and are used by permission of the copyright owner. All rights reserved. No part of the New American Bible may be reproduced in any form without permission in writing from the copyright owner.

Every reasonable effort has been made to determine copyright holders of excerpted materials and to secure permissions as needed. If any copyrighted materials have been inadvertently used in this work without proper credit being given in one form or another, please notify Our Sunday Visitor in writing so that future printings of this work may be corrected accordingly.

Our Sunday Visitor Publishing Division, Our Sunday Visitor, Inc., 200 Noll Plaza, Huntington, IN 46750, www.osv.com; 1-800-348-2440.

ISBN: 978-1-68192-432-8 (Inventory No. T2321)

1. RELIGION—Christian Education—General.
2. RELIGION—Christian Ministry—Pastoral Resources.
3. RELIGION—Christianity—Catholic.

eISBN: 978-1-68192-433-5
LCCN: 2020939437

Cover and interior design: Amanda Falk
Cover art: Christ the True Vine icon G. Dagli Orti /De Agostini Picture Library / Bridgeman Images

PRINTED IN THE UNITED STATES OF AMERICA

*This book is dedicated to Professor
Barbara A. Morgan (1938–2019)
Generous mentor, dear friend,
and master catechist*

Contents

Contents

Foreword

To become a Catholic, for me, was to find out how much I didn't know.

Seen from the outside, Catholicism seems pretty simple. It looks like the last movie you saw with a minor character who's a priest. It looks like the guy you met at the bowling alley who mentioned his parish fish fry in passing. It's not impressive at all. In fact, it's hardly worth remembering.

I was genuinely surprised by how much bigger the Church was on the inside. *I had not known* the reach of Catholic charity and relief efforts in my own town — never mind in the world! I had not known that there was a seemingly infinite variety of expressions of spirituality — Ignatian, Teresian, Theresian, Byzantine, Charismatic, Benedictine, Augustinian. ... Every day I read books whose footnotes alerted me to authors previously unknown, and I assumed that every Catholic must know them.

Here I was with an advanced degree in theology and almost

done with another, and I felt like it was all useless paper. I had been majoring in minor things since my youth, gaining knowledge that had no application in my new world. I had pursued a career that dead-ended with my conversion.

I called up a Catholic friend who was extremely well educated and widely cultured, and I put the question to him: Did I have any future as a Catholic theologian? He assured me that I did not. To be a Catholic theologian, he explained, required command of many ancient and modern languages and mastery of entire schools of thought whose very names were only vaguely familiar to me.

Well, that was that.

My next call was to my father, and I asked him if I could have a job working the counter in his jewelry shop. He was even less encouraging. The whole country was suffering through a recession. Nobody was buying diamond rings and wristwatches.

So I settled into my chair and pondered. I had no desire to sell jewelry, anyway, so that was just as well. What I wanted to do was teach people about Jesus Christ — about the Scriptures — about the Church. Yet, I agreed with my discouraging friend that I had no right to call myself a Catholic theologian. That would be pretentious beyond measure.

So maybe I could be something else: a catechist.

I loved the sound of that word. It was another one of those new Catholic terms for me. No one in my evangelical world held that title. Among Calvinists there was the *Geneva Catechism,* and then the *Westminster Shorter Catechism* and the *Westminster Larger Catechism.* But, except for the clergy, we had no cohort of people who were charged and commissioned to teach the doctrine in those books.

Catechist. It sounded exotic, and its Greek roots were redolent of Christian antiquity.

I liked it. It would be my future.

That moment was pivotal for me. It was formative. It set the course for my professional life.

In spite of my friend's discouraging words, I did become a Catholic theologian. But I hope I've never ceased to be a catechist — a teacher of the principles of Christian religion.

In everything I've done professionally since that long-ago moment in that armchair, I've tried to make the truths and mysteries of Christianity intelligible to as wide a swath of people as possible. Yes, I've written a bit for my colleagues in academia, but even then I've striven never to tune out or turn off my neighbors in my parish.

Early on, I found good models for this. I discovered the great teachers of the ancient catechetical schools: Pantaenus, Clement, and Origen. And I pored over the great mystagogues — Cyril, Ambrose, Augustine, and Chrysostom — who revealed the hidden magnitude of the Church's sacraments. If I have failed as a catechist, it's not because I didn't aim high.

Along the way, I learned an important and reassuring lesson: Everybody needs a catechist. Even catechists need to be catechized. Even theologians need to be catechized. We all need to revisit and review the basics. We all need to be as practiced in listening and learning as we are in lecturing and teaching.

In fact, we all need to see ourselves always in the midst of conversion — a conversion that is ongoing and never ends. We are not just making converts. We *are* converts, even if we've been Catholics since the cradle.

James Pauley knows this. He has a sense of the profound dignity of the vocation of catechist. At the same time, he understands the profound humility that is necessary in the person of the catechist.

Our great dignity and our utter unworthiness: Unless we keep a healthy sense of both, we'll be lost. And the only way to do that is through an authentic life of piety. Fruitful catechesis depends upon catechists who live in Trinitarian communion — catechists who sustain an intentional, disciplined life of prayer and sacramental participation.

Dr. Pauley has written this book for that very purpose. It's a practical handbook — a *vademecum* — that can go with us everywhere and always enrich us, so that we can always enrich the people we serve.

Seen from the inside, the Church is vast, and we will never know all that can be known about it. But between the covers of this book, we can find what we need to know and thrive as catechists.

Scott Hahn, PhD
March 2020

Author's Note

Each chapter of this book includes stories from some remarkable parents, catechists, Catholic school teachers, and catechetical leaders from around North America. It is my hope that these testimonies will inspire and challenge readers as much as they have me.

Part I

The Encounter with Christ

Gandalf the Grey has always been a favorite literary character of mine. In J. R. R. Tolkien's masterful tale *The Lord of the Rings*, the wizard Gandalf is sent to Middle-earth to help its inhabitants — both the small and the great — to stand against growing darkness. Gandalf moves hobbits, elves, dwarves, men, and women to heroic action. He does this not so much by his power as a wizard, but by rousing them out of their complacency and fear, setting before them the urgency of what they must do in the battle against evil. By Gandalf's influence, key characters discover their courage and, through the assiduous work of taking small steps forward, realize greatness. There are others, however, who remain absorbed within themselves, failing to grow into who they must become.

A pivotal moment in the narrative comes as Gandalf liberates King Théoden of Rohan from his interior darkness. Théoden's only son has been recently killed in battle, and he himself has long been influenced to inaction by the craven counsel of a particularly treacherous advisor. As a result, Théoden has failed to mobilize his people for the coming battle that is nearly at his doorstep. His inaction, if not immediately remedied, would be disastrous. Gandalf engages the king with stirring words:

> "Now Théoden son of Thengel, will you hearken to me?" said Gandalf. "Do you ask for help?" He lifted his staff and pointed to a high window. There the darkness seemed to clear, and through the opening could be seen, high and far, a patch of shining sky. "Not all is dark. Take courage, Lord of the Mark; for better help you will not find. No counsel have I to give to those that despair. Yet counsel I could give, and words I could speak to you. Will you hear them? They are not for all ears. I bid you come out before

your doors and look abroad. Too long have you
sat in shadows and trusted to twisted tales and
crooked promptings."[1]

What, you might be wondering, does Gandalf the wizard have to
do with your work as a catechist? As we share the precious content of the Faith that God wants each person to receive, those we
teach also have to be awakened. Our students must be interiorly
moved and inspired as they are taught. They must be convicted
that the radically new way of seeing offered them by Jesus is not
dry, uninteresting, or disconnected from their life; but is, in fact,
critical to correctly understanding the travails and attractions
of our fallen world. The light of the Gospel is necessary to find
lasting joy and to realize the purposes for which we have been
created.

Every catechist is indispensable to this awakening needed in
the Church today.

[1] J. R. R. Tolkien, *The Two Towers* (New York: Ballantine Books, 1988), 140–41.

CHAPTER ONE

The Catechist and the Quest for Fruitfulness

How can our catechesis move the heart and awaken the mind? What would it look like for us to teach in ways that stir up a lifelong desire for God and a vibrant Catholic life of generous, self-sacrificing love? What must we do to be fruitful in this most important work?

Catechesis today cannot be carried out successfully in a ho-hum, business-as-usual, mediocre fashion. We are privileged to live and teach in a defining, critical moment in world history, and these times require catechetical approaches that are laser-focused on calling learners to nothing less than real discipleship.

Heroic missionaries throughout the centuries have faced adversity at least as great as ours. This has required of them a willingness to sacrifice, courage to accept the risk of apparent failure, and sometimes even a readiness to suffer and die on account of teaching the Gospel. We remember Saint Francis Xavier and his spiritual sons bringing Christ to a very dangerous sixteenth-century Japan, or Saint Teresa of Calcutta and her spiritual daughters serving the poor in places overwhelmed by poverty and disease. Francis reputedly said to those who were forming young Jesuits in Europe at the time, "Tell the students to give up their small ambitions and come eastward to preach the Gospel of Christ."[1] And Saint Teresa of Calcutta put it this way: "We have to carry Our Lord to places where he has not walked before. Therefore, the sisters must be consumed with one desire: Jesus. Speak of no one but him crucified. We must not be afraid to do the things he did — to go fearlessly through death and danger with him and for him."[2] These two great saints embraced their challenging work out of a love for God and a desire for the highest good — eternal joy in heaven! — of each individual person to whom they were sent.

Today's catechist is also a missionary, though not usually in the sense of traveling to distant lands. Rather, we offer the content of the Gospel to people who live near us, yet who ex-

---

[1] These words, widely attributed to Saint Francis Xavier, are perhaps a paraphrase of words he wrote to his superiors in a letter in 1543: "It often comes into my mind to go round all the universities of Europe, and especially that of Paris, crying out everywhere like a madman, and saying to all the learned men there whose learning is so much greater than their charity, 'Ah! What a multitude of souls is through your fault shut out of heaven and falling into hell! Would to God that these men who labour so much in gaining knowledge would give as much thought to the account they must one day give to God of the use they have made of their learning and of the talents entrusted to them!" He continues a little later in the same letter, "I declare to God that I had almost made up my mind, since I could not return to Europe myself, to write to the University of Paris, and especially to our worthy Professors Cornet and Picard, and to show them how many thousands of infidels might be made Christians without trouble, if we had only men here who would seek, not their own advantage, but the things of Jesus Christ. And therefore, dearest brothers, 'pray ye the Lord of the harvest that he send forth labourers into his harvest' (Mt 25:20)." Henry James Coleridge, *The Life and Letters of Saint Francis Xavier*, vol. 1 (London: Burns and Oates, 1872), 156–57, https://archive.org/details /LifeLettersOfStFrancisXavierV1/page/n187, accessed November 11, 2019.

[2] Angelo Devananda, ed., *Total Surrender: Mother Teresa* (Ann Arbor, MI: Servant, 1990), 141.

perience cultural influences increasingly foreign to Christianity. Catechists who have taught for several decades know that today we teach in particularly unstable circumstances, as compared with even ten years ago. Many of those we form are growing up in families who expect very little of their children (or of themselves) when it comes to prayer and sacramental practice. These families, irreplaceable in the formation of Christians, are sometimes indifferent or even hostile to helping young people become real disciples of Christ. The broader society in which young Christians are being formed is rapidly abandoning the firm footing of objective truth and reality. The Church herself seems, for many, to have lost her moral authority. And many parishes struggle to provide an authentic Christian community where individuals are known and loved by people of faith.

THE ONLY WAY FORWARD

In anticipation of the Great Jubilee Year 2000, Holy Cross College in Notre Dame, Indiana, constructed a majestic Jubilee arch on its campus. Across the arch is etched the motto: Ave Crux Spes Unica ("Hail to the Cross, our only hope"). These words reflect the interior attunement of the true follower of Jesus. The disciple's graced instinct — especially when facing adversity — is to root himself more and more in Christ, crucified and risen from the dead. In him alone do we find our hope.

This rootedness in Christ, seen in so many of the heroic missionaries of the past, is the same disposition we need today. Catechist-missionaries must accept that their own identity as disciples of Christ is the essential foundation for their teaching. Saint John Paul II, in fact, took this point to its logical conclusion when he explained that "the true missionary is the saint."[3]

---

[3] Quoted in Congregation for the Evangelization of Peoples, *Guide for Catechists*, accessed April 20, 2020, Vatican.va, art. 6

With this insight, John Paul II brings us to this most important link between who we are and what we teach.

What are we missionary-catechists to do with his words? Of course, we would agree that ideally, we should be saints. But we are so keenly aware of our own weaknesses, our own sinfulness, and how frequently we stand in need of God's mercy. Sometimes our halfheartedness undermines and diminishes what we give to this work for God. Do John Paul's words disqualify us, then, from being catechists? Or should we simply acknowledge the nobility of his idea, while dismissing it as a bit idealistic? "After all," we might think to ourselves, "it's easy for him to say. He actually was a saint!"

Sainthood is not a prerequisite for our work, but the serious commitment to our own growth in holiness is. If we want our catechesis to be fruitful, this commitment to holiness must be our life's orientation. This is why Jesus said to the Church's very first catechists-in-training, the apostles, "As the Father loves me, so I also love you. Remain in my love" (Jn 15:9). Thus, before we turn to the question of how to teach in an evangelizing way (Part II of this book), we must first closely examine the unique vocation each of us has to become rooted in God.

So many heroic men and women missionaries of past centuries carried out their work deeply aware of their poverty before their mission and their great need to remain in God. This poverty caused them to take daily measures to anchor their work in a life of communion with God. Looking again to our brother Francis Xavier and sister Teresa of Calcutta: Francis desired his brother Jesuits to found their missionary work in the profound experience of the spiritual exercises of Saint Ignatius Loyola. Teresa set the mark for her sisters by beginning each day with the Mass and a Eucharistic holy hour. Through committed habits, these courageous missionaries strove to remain in close communion with the Lord and with their communities, to the great good of those they served. Indeed, it was through this everyday investment in their life in Christ, as well as in the extreme demands of their missionary work, that they grew by stages in sanctity, ever so gradually being perfected in Christlike love. So, too, must it be for you and me and all of today's missionary catechists, if we are seeking to be fruitful.

CATECHESIS: A VOCATION

Catechesis isn't merely a task for which a person volunteers or a job for which a person trains. Moreover, it should not be a responsibility assigned to just anyone. The Church calls catechesis a vocation. It is a calling from God. On account of the great need represented in the people whom the catechist forms and the immeasurable beauty of the content of Revelation that the catechist teaches, the work of the catechist is infinitely valuable.

Therefore, God chooses to invite imperfect, finite human beings to this vital work of forming disciples through catechesis. This invitation comes to us individually — even personally. When we faithfully respond to this invitation, being a catechist is a sure way to holiness. In fact, God delights in sanctifying each of us as we teach. For this reason, catechesis is a saint-making experience, as much for the catechist as it is for the catechized.

Francis Xavier and Teresa of Calcutta grew in daily sanctity by bringing Christ to the people they encountered, and this can be true for us as well. Whatever our current thresholds are for loving God, embracing the content of the Church's teaching, and pouring ourselves out for the good of those we teach, these thresholds will be stretched and deepened through our cooperation with Christ. Catechesis thus becomes an experience of Christ first working in us so that he can work through us, all to the greater glory of God.

Beth Spizarny of Ann Arbor, Michigan, gives us a glimpse into what growing in holiness as a catechist looks like in her life, particularly in a challenging experience she had giving a presentation on an adult retreat:

> No one brags about how weak they are. Everyone wants to think of themselves as confident, capable, self-sufficient … *strong*. I certainly don't recall being cheered on for how physically weak I was as a freshman in gym class! And if there had been an award for that, I certainly would have won. I couldn't bench press *the bar*. These are not the stories we celebrate or share with others — we love sharing the stories in which we were the heroes.
>
> The paradox of the Christian faith is that when we are weak, God's greatness and his strength are made manifest. Saint Paul begged the Lord to take away a thorn in his side, but the response was *"My grace is sufficient for you, for power is made perfect in weakness"* (2 Cor 12:9).
>
> Over many years in ministry, I have been drawn to a deeper union with God on many occasions. Frequently, this comes through a powerful experience of my weakness.
>
> It was a simple talk, intended to bring to culmination a one-day retreat experience for sixty adults. The retreat focused on the Person of the Holy Spirit and the invitation to surrender to God. Often this retreat is a turning point in people's lives, as they experience God in a personal way for the first time! The days leading up to the retreat were challenging. My talk was replacing a video, since the retreat already included four other videos. Reviewing the lengthy

outline from the video, I could hardly bear to cut any of the suggested content; yet, squeezing it all in felt clunky and unnatural. After many hours, I felt frustrated.

Early in the morning on the day of the retreat, a friend encouraged me to ask the Lord for the freedom to put the content into my own words. As I heard her words, I knew that the Lord had intervened and spoken to me through her. Instantly I felt free! With the incredible amount of time I had already spent poring over the material, ordering the few, essential things I felt called to include took just a few minutes.

Unfortunately, to my surprise, somehow throughout the retreat day, old wounds resurfaced. With just five minutes before I was supposed to offer the talk, I was barely holding back the tears. For many reasons, I felt alone and forgotten by God. Turning to two leaders, I asked them to pray with me. I explained that I had just five minutes before offering the final talk, and that I felt like a total mess. To my great disappointment, I even began to cry. With incredible tenderness, they began to pray and invite the Holy Spirit to free me and empower me to share God's message. What a great change I experienced! They had barely finished praying when they announced my name from the front. As I walked to the podium, I knew that I was weak — but I also knew the Lord was with me. I wasn't alone; I wasn't forgotten.

The sensation of God's presence and desire to speak through me was palpable. I saw his love for the people in that room. The words that God spoke through me were beautiful, challenging, and invitational. The heart of the message was that following him isn't complicated — it's simply saying yes to him now, and in all the "nows" that will come. I shared about how my son has a favorite Spider-Man T-shirt that he wears constantly, until I can manage to get the filthy thing off of him after many days and nights. I explained that in the same way, the Lord wants to take the rubbish out of our own lives to give us something clean, something beautiful. I challenged people to keep saying yes, to keep inviting the Lord to come into their lives and lead them.

It was a powerful talk, and the reality of my own weakness made it even more marvelous. The two leaders who had prayed with me knew how directly God had intervened to speak to everyone through me that night.

An image that comes to mind is that of a kite: The flimsy things are caught up by a powerful wind, soaring to incredible heights. In our weakness, God is glorified. Saint Paul proclaimed, "If I must boast, I will boast of the things that show my weakness" (2 Cor 11:30). Let's be weak, that God might bring us to incredible heights for the glory of his name.

God allows the inevitable challenges we face in this work — from sparse resources to participants who seem indifferent to a sometimes overwhelming awareness of our own limitations — so that we might be stirred to greater virtue and radical trust in his providential care. The Lord Jesus intends, through our cooperation with him in his catechetical mission, to form us to be catechetical saints who, like the Beloved Apostle at the Last Supper, lean into the heart of Christ. Deacon James Keating explains, "[A] catechist is someone who desires to rest upon the heart of Christ and to receive all that he wishes to give from that heart."[4] This process unfolds as we come to know him more deeply and rely on him in our own need. And it is being accomplished in us as we gladly propose the content of his mystery.

The content of the Faith is an extraordinary treasure we have the privilege to pass on to people, and they will perceive the Faith as the treasure that meets their deepest needs when it is communicated with love and deep personal conviction. Pope Saint Paul VI once wrote, "Modern man listens more willingly to witnesses than to teachers, and if he does listen to teachers it is because they are witnesses."[5] Catechists who give witness to a life lived in Christ are critically important to the spiritual development of those they form.

THE WITNESS OF PARENTS

There is no relationship more instrumental in the Catholic life than the one between parent and child. We see this clearly in families where there is a lack of love and faith, and in extreme cases where children are abused and neglected. But we also see the positive effects of this relationship in families where faith and the call to discipleship lovingly animate the home. Therefore, we shouldn't proceed in this book without mentioning just how important parents are to this work of an evangelizing catechesis. This is the case not only in childhood; a parent's living faith can be impactful throughout a child's adult life, too. Be-

---

[4] James Keating, "Teaching Out of Our Desire for God," *The Catechetical Review* 2, no. 2 (April 2016): 10.

[5] Paul VI, *Evangelii Nuntiandi,* accessed April 20, 2020, Vatican.va, par. 41.

cause of the significant role parents must fulfill in the mission of catechesis, the ideas discussed in these chapters are intended not only for catechetical leaders and catechists, but for parents, who are our primary catechists.

The parental influence is deep and broad. Memorable impressions are frequently made in the simplest of exchanges. Just ask Sister Patricia McCormack, IHM, who remembers a striking conversation she had around the dinner table with her parents when she was a young girl:

> What do you remember of your first day of grade one? My memory gave prophetic purpose and lifelong value to my life! After taking roll and assigning seats to her 120 students (not a typographical error!), petite Sister St. Rose announced that our first lesson would be the most important lesson of our lives. She distributed our first catechism book and directed us to lesson one. With pencil in hand, we circled question numbers one, two, and three. Sister instructed us in the meaning of the words and told us to have our parents teach us how to say the words with our eyes closed.
>
> My mother proctored homework time. She amazed me when, without looking at the book, she knew the answers to the three questions. More amazing yet was dinner conversation that night. Mom said, "Pat, tell Dad what you learned at school today." I looked my dad straight in the eye and declared with conviction, "I learned why God made me." Without skipping a beat, my father proclaimed, "Pat, God made you to know him, to love him, and to serve him in this

> world, and to be happy with him forever in the
> next." Dad's reply had an exponential influence
> because ... Dad's misbehaviors were legendary,
> and yearly Santa Claus deposited coal in his
> stocking because of it. So, when this man knew
> why God made me, I embraced the belief hook,
> line, and sinker![6]

Even in very ordinary conversations, parents have so much influence. It is also true that in times of real adversity and suffering in the family, much can be learned about the Christian life from loving parents. Adam and Christy Demuro of Phoenix, Arizona, have a young son, Paul, who has cancer. In these difficult circumstances, as they all suffer with Paul, conversations arise with their children that are deeply formative and infinitely valuable. Christy describes one of these:

> Yesterday, Paul wanted his older brother Sam-
> my to come with him when he went to the hos-
> pital for treatment. But Sammy was worried
> about saying "yes" because he would fall behind
> on his schoolwork, particularly his math. Here's
> what I told Sammy: "Sammy, at the hospital you
> will learn about math, particularly if you pay at-
> tention to the mathematical equations used to
> analyze Paul's blood counts and to determine
> proper chemotherapy doses. You will learn sci-
> ence as you watch modern medicine and chem-
> icals keep your brother alive in the face of an
> illness that, in the not-too-distant past, was con-

---

[6] Sr. Patricia M. McCormack, IHM, "Children's Catechesis: Forming a Culture of Prayer within the Home," *The Catechetical Review* 4, no. 4 (October 2018): 30.

sidered a death sentence. You will learn com-
passion as you walk with your brother through
his struggles. You will learn sacrifice as you give
your brother any toy or game of yours that he
wants, to help ease his suffering. You will learn
courage as your brother bravely faces medical
treatments that cause pain or discomfort. You
will learn solidarity as you take upon yourself
the pain and the risks of vaccinations, in order
to protect your immunocompromised brother
from illnesses that would be potentially fatal to
him. You will learn to live the works of mercy,
particularly to comfort the sorrowful and to
visit the sick. And you will learn love, which is
the most important thing in our family."

For Catholics, parenthood is a vocation. This call from God includes the responsibility to be the first catechist for one's own
children. Parents who take this charge to heart can help their
kids come to know God as he gives himself in the sacramental
life. They can form them from an early age in the virtues. And
they can equip them with the discernment skills that will see
them through life's uncertain and dark periods. They will also be
best able to answer that question of why authority over one's life
should be given to God. Yet, many catechists reading this book
will understandably be uneasy, because parish and school reality
shows us that most parents do not prioritize becoming missionary disciples themselves, let alone being the primary catechists
for their own children. Sadly, this problem isn't going away soon.

This means we as catechists must also focus our energies on
stirring up a desire for God in parents and on helping them form
a culture of discipleship within their home. Why? A few years
ago, the University of Notre Dame made available a very helpful

study by sociologists Christian Smith and Lisa Pearce that convincingly demonstrates why we must put the parent-child catechetical relationship first. The study itself sought to determine the factors in the home that influence young people to continue to practice their faith into young adulthood. Perhaps the greatest takeaway from the National Survey of Youth and Religion was summarized in a 2017 article:

> Of the most religious quartile of NSYR young adults ages 24–29 … an impressive 82 percent had parents who reported each of the following: that their family regularly talked about religious topics in the home, that faith was "very important" to them, and that they themselves regularly were involved in religious activities. By comparison, only 1 percent of the least religious quartile of … young adults had parents who reported this combination of religious attitudes and practices. Thus, according to the [study], the single most decisive difference between Millennials who remained religiously committed into adulthood and those who didn't was the degree of religiousness exhibited by their parents.[7]

It is clear that, for us as catechists, helping parents has to become our most important priority. This includes not only helping them become "involved in religious activities" and to feel their

---

[7] Justin Bartkus, "The Home: A Catholic Subculture that Makes a Difference," *The Catechetical Review* 3, no. 2 (April 2017): 9–11, emphasis author's. More information on the study can be found at www.youthandreligion.nd.edu (accessed November 11, 2019). A fascinating overview of the importance of this study may be viewed at https://www.youtube.com/watch?v=v0FzwlM5iLM (accessed November 11, 2019).

faith to be "very important," but also assisting them to frequently talk with their kids about what life in Christ means and why it is infinitely valuable. For catechetical leaders and catechists, helping parents encounter Jesus in a transforming way, and strengthening the catechetical relationship between parent and child, is worth every effort and sacrifice. There is nothing more important for our catechetical ministries.

What can we do to inspire and encourage parents in their own Catholic faith and life? How do we help parents to establish or deepen a dynamic culture of Catholic life and conversation in the home? How do we empower them in the catechesis of their own children? When parents are encouraged — often by other parents — to take steps to live a life of faith and to personally invest in their children's discipleship, children will receive the very best foundation for a dynamic Catholic life of following Jesus in the Church. They also, consequently, are more likely to remain committed Catholics as they enter adulthood.

THE CATECHIST: REMAINING IN CHRIST

The catechist-disciple cannot live only from an encounter with God that happened earlier in life. Rather, the catechist must stand as a living witness, choosing to teach from a posture of continual encounter with God. Teaching from this posture begins even as we prepare to teach.

I see this posture of encounter frequently in my students as they prepare to serve the Church in the catechetical field. My theology and catechetics students at Franciscan University of Steubenville show me how preparing for their mission as catechetical leaders sanctifies them. Victoria Vas, one of my former students who now teaches in a Catholic high school, described the personal conversion she experienced as she prepared to teach about the Lord's Day as an assignment in my class:

I have often heard that a teacher must also be a learner. This especially goes for catechists, who must sit at the feet of the Christ, the One True Teacher. Yet, it wasn't until I taught the topic of the Lord's Day that I actually lived this, and was more deeply evangelized through planning and teaching the lesson.

I drew the central message of my lesson, "Put not your trust in princes" from Psalm 146, and formed my entire lesson around this truth that the highest action we can perform as humans is to worship. To do so forms in us a deeper trust and hope in the Lord, not in worldly things. A primary way in which God calls us to worship is by participating in Sunday Mass, and then entrusting our entire Sundays to him, as days of rest and leisure. I couldn't in good conscience teach this without trying to live it out, so from the start of the semester I began setting aside Sundays as days of leisure, free of homework assignments and studying. Instead of working, I began taking that time to do things I can't normally do during the week, such as spending time with friends, going on hikes, or painting. In simply taking one day out of the week for wholesome leisure, I found myself rejuvenated for the rest of the week of work, and in striving to protect my day of rest, I was more motivated to concentrate and study diligently during the week. Furthermore, I used the time I set aside each Sunday during that semester to paint a canvas inscribed with "Put not your trust in princes." The hours I spent working on it were not only enjoyable and relaxing, but

prayerful moments in which I was able to dwell
on the truth of the Lord's Day, and let it take root
in my heart. In a beautiful way, I found myself
falling more deeply in love with Christ by my
work of catechesis.

Now that Victoria is a full-time teacher and not just a teacher in
training, she undoubtedly finds it more challenging to deeply
reflect like this on everything she teaches. But her experience
nevertheless demonstrates what it means to allow the Faith we
teach to evangelize and form us. Every time we teach, we are
afforded opportunities to grow as disciples, to be transfigured in
how we ourselves think and live. The crucial prerequisite is that
we are catechists who are attuned to the One who also wants to
teach us and conform us to himself.

That is why this book begins with an emphasis on being before doing. In the following chapters, we will look first to the
relationship that the catechist-disciple enjoys with God, exploring two important ways of encountering God: in moments of
authentic prayer, and through a vibrant sacramental life. It is
primarily through these two postures of encounter that the catechist is able to credibly teach others the Christian Faith and how
to live life to its fullest as disciples being transformed in Christ.

CHAPTER TWO

Prayer
The Soul of Our Teaching

I grew up in the southwestern desert of the United States, so I'm quite familiar with the dry washes that pervade Arizona's arid landscape. In the spring when the snows in the mountains melt, these washes surge with waters. But it is not long before the waters slow to a trickle as their sources in the mountains are exhausted. Eventually, they become streambeds of dry sand, meandering memorials to the vigor and zeal of those first weeks of spring.

How familiar this reality is in the spiritual life of many catechists. Catechists so frequently extend themselves in generosity, giving their passion to this work. Unfortunately, reassuring signs that they are making a difference in the lives of those they teach can be infrequent or nonexistent. If catechists cannot draw from inner depths sustained by the living waters welling up within that the Lord promised to the Samaritan woman (cf. Jn 4:14), they will not be able to maintain their passion for long. Each Christian wishing to give substantively to others must draw from the depths of the spiritual life himself.

"If you are wise," writes the great Saint Bernard of Clairvaux, "you will be reservoirs and not channels." Spiritual writer Jean-Baptiste Chautard explains: "The channels let the water flow away, and do not retain a drop. But the reservoir is first filled, and then, without emptying itself, pours out its overflow, which is ever renewed, over the fields which it waters."[1] Chautard continues: "How many there are devoted to works, who are never anything but channels, and retain nothing for themselves, but remain dry while trying to pass on life-giving grace to souls!"[2] The advice, then, of Saint Bernard and Jean-Baptiste Chautard? Be filled with God. Prioritize communion with him. This is especially necessary for those responsible for introducing others to that living water who is Christ: parents, pastors, catechists. When we ourselves draw upon this deep reservoir of communion with God, we are able to give ourselves over time to the apostolate of helping others receive these life-giving waters.

Chances are, you picked up this book because you want to be a better communicator of the Faith. You want those you teach to respond to Christ's great proposal with a resounding, lifelong "Yes!" What is it that makes such a response possible in our students? We might be tempted to come up with a list of abilities we try to bring to our catechesis. Perhaps we think it is our personal level of conviction regarding the content of the

---

[1] Jean-Baptiste Chautard, OCSO, *The Soul of the Apostolate* (Charlotte, NC: TAN Books, 1946), 55. The words of Saint Bernard may be found in Sermons on the Song of Songs
[2] Ibid.

Faith and our own creativity that make us effective. Or maybe it is our attempts to build relationships and rapport with those we teach. Or perhaps it's our speaking ability or our knowledge of the cultural influences in which our students live. Or maybe it's our ability to make them laugh. As important as our personal talents and teaching methods are, they are not the source of our effectiveness.

Rather, we must turn first to an even more fundamental and mysterious wellspring. To effectively lead those we teach to communion with God, we must attend to the depth and quality of our own union with him in prayer. As a soul gives life to a body, so too will our own communion with God animate and empower our teaching. Fruitfulness in teaching can only be achieved in God — through him, with him, and in him. Our natural creative capacities are, on their own, radically insufficient to this mission. Perhaps, with me, you find such an acknowledgment to be liberating. Simply put, we need God.

With Saint John Paul II, we can also say this about the catechist's prayer life: "Unless the missionary is a contemplative, he cannot proclaim Christ in a credible way."[3] It is our own life in God that will make us believable guides in the way of Christ.

UNION WITH CHRIST: THE NECESSARY INGREDIENT

Union with Christ was important for the seventy-two disciples whom the Lord sent out in pairs to proclaim the Kingdom of God. They returned from this mission rejoicing, having experienced considerable fruit in their proclamation of the kingdom (cf. Lk 10:1–20). Of course, their connection with the Lord was profound, as they knew themselves to have been appointed and

---

[3] John Paul II, *Redemptoris Missio*, accessed April 20, 2020, Vatican.va, par. 91. The *Catechism's* treatment of contemplation is well worth reading, to better understand what Saint John Paul II means. See especially CCC 2709–2719.

sent by him.

Perhaps there is no more compelling biblical example of a disciple being in union with Christ and experiencing fruitfulness as a teacher than that of Saint Peter. Late in the Gospel of John, Peter appears to be a different man after professing three times to the Risen One, "Lord, you know that I love you!" After each of these professions of his love, the Lord charges Peter to "feed my sheep" (Jn 21:15–17). We see here the profound dependence of Peter's mission upon his closeness to Christ. We also see with what tenderness Christ extends this opportunity for healing: one restorative confession of love for each of Peter's denials during Jesus' trial. This event of extraordinary vulnerability and intimacy conformed Peter deeply to the Master he loved. The mission he was given was rooted in this profession of love and also in his certainty of the Master's union with him. Once he received the divine gift of the Holy Spirit on Pentecost, Peter was able to stand with his fellow apostles, deep in communion with God, and fearlessly proclaim the Gospel. "You who are Jews, indeed all of you staying in Jerusalem. Let this be known to you, and listen to my words" (Acts 2:14). The fruit that accompanied his first catechesis in the subsequent verses must have surprised him. After all, just weeks earlier Peter had been nearly overcome by fear and self-reprehension. As his hearers were "cut to the heart," asking, "What are we to do, my brothers?" perhaps Peter, too, was more deeply cut to the heart by the grace of God alive in him and working through him (cf. Acts 2:37).

Every person has a deep need to be formed in the Faith by catechist-disciples who truly know the Lord and are able to live as witnesses to the joy of the Gospel. For us, we might look back on our own experience of being formed by our most influential catechists and see that it was truly Christ alive in them who ignited our curiosity and deepened our desire for God. On the other hand, we might not have received a compelling witness from our catechists in our most formative years. For far too many young people, this lack of witness contributes to their loss of interest in the Faith. But in some situations — perhaps our own — knowing that something essential is missing can provoke questions and needs that eventually propel a person toward Jesus. Thanks be to God when he brings such good out of a situation of poverty.

The catechist's spiritual life, then, enlivens catechesis like nothing else can. The disciple-catechist becomes more and more convincing as the integrity between his faith and life increases. For catechists who intently pursue holiness of life, how we think, act, love, serve others, suffer, pray, and worship becomes, through our communion with Christ, more harmonious with what we teach. We then become inspiring teachers of the Faith — frequently unbeknownst to us — because the fruits of our life in Christ have an attractive power. As we become more transparent to Christ alive in us, more conformed to him through a life of ongoing conversion, the possibility increases that our students will meet him in us, because he is truly alive in us.

What does this pursuit of holiness look like for catechists and teachers today? Here is one account from a first-time Catholic schoolteacher, as she faced difficulty in her first few months of teaching. Jessica Schuster of Swanton, Ohio, writes:

> I graduated from my Catholic university committed to a relationship with Jesus Christ. My relationship with him had been nourished by daily Mass and daily prayer time before the Blessed Sacrament, strengthened through challenges, protected by self-discipline and habit, supported by friends in the same state of striving, and bolstered by constant reminders from my professors that we could not give to others

what we did not have ourselves. In short, I was confident that I would be entering the field with a solid (even, perhaps, an unshakable) spiritual life.

Just weeks before my December graduation, I was asked by a pastor to consider a teaching position at his school that had unexpectedly become available. After spending much time in prayer and discernment, I felt that the Lord was calling me to take the job and that his grace would supply for what I lacked in experience. Two weeks after I was hired, the spring semester began.

There were difficulties almost immediately. In addition to the challenges of being a first-time teacher, which I expected, I experienced conflict with another faculty member that I could not have foreseen. I was deeply shaken; for the first time in my life, I felt like an utter failure, and began to doubt the Lord and myself. Surely I had made a mistake in discerning that this job was the Lord's will for me ... and yet, I had asked him to show me his will, and he had made clear this path for me. Where was his hand in this? In my misery and distrust, I began to fold in upon myself and let go of my spiritual moorings. I decided I had neither the time nor the energy to attend daily Mass at the end of the school day. Even though I knew I should have been running to the Lord to let him console and guide me, I soon stopped taking time to listen to his voice.

By the end of the school year, I was a mess — physically, emotionally, and spiritually. I had decided not to return to my teaching position, and as I faced my unknown future, I realized that I could not truly discern and hear the Lord's will for my life unless I set aside the time to be with him and let my heart grow accustomed once again to the sound of his voice above all others. I wrote in my journal:

My Resolutions Moving Forward
- Daily Mass
- Daily Holy Hour — NO EXCEPTIONS

Over the next several weeks, I really strived to be faithful to my resolutions. I went to daily Mass and sat alone afterward in front of the tabernacle, opening myself to his voice by reading his word in Sacred Scripture. The current of his presence and his peace began flowing through my soul, and I remember thinking, how could I have ever lived without this, without this daily communion with him? This is not to say that the hard circumstances of my job — the challenges of first-time teaching and difficulties with my colleague — would not have existed, if only I had been faithful to my relationship with Christ. I knew that the situation itself would not have changed; but if I had taken the time to rest against his Heart in prayer, I would have been strengthened to meet those challenges in peace, confidence, and trust.

I grew to realize that this teaching job had been allowed by Christ the Teacher to utterly convince me of his words, "As the branch cannot bear fruit by itself, unless it abides in the vine, neither can you, unless you abide in me."

In my pride and naivety, I had never thought that I would compromise my prayer life. Yet there I was, choosing to go at my difficult ministry "by myself" and, to a certain degree, "apart" from him … and I had found the joy, peace, love, and life within me rapidly withering away. To my amazement and eventual joy, I saw that my teaching job had not only been beneficial to my ongoing conversion as a catechist and my personal relationship with Jesus Christ … it had been necessary. For if we catechists are not convinced — utterly convinced — and living the conviction that apart from him we can do nothing, how can our ministry bear fruit?

As I continue my catechetical work today, my daily communion with Christ remains the lifeblood of all my efforts. Any time I start to grow slack in my commitment to prayer and find excuses to prioritize other things above my daily time with him, I find that I am externally carrying out the responsibilities of my ministry, but my perspective has shifted from doing the Lord's work for the Lord, to doing my work for me. I discover that I become overly concerned with winning the approval of others, discouraged, proud, restless, weary, and afraid of failure. But thankfully, the Lord in his patience does not tire of teaching me the same lesson over and over again. Without him, I can do nothing.

Being a missionary disciple and catechist who prioritizes a deep relationship with Jesus will make us stand out. Sherry Weddell describes such Christians as those who live curiously: "The Catholic life is to be a 'sign of contradiction' in this world ... [This] means we are to live lives of such inexplicable joy, love, faith, and peace (even in trial) that all the normal categories by which nonbelievers try to classify us won't work."[4] When such a person is the one forming others in the Faith, curiosity and desire can arise for what the catechist teaches. This curiosity, of course, rarely shows itself in our students immediately, expert as so many are at keeping such things hidden and below the surface. But the more the fruits of the Holy Spirit shine through catechists who live in prayerful communion with God, the more they will wonder what and who it is that makes us different.

An interior life anchored to the Blessed Trinity will sustain perseverance amidst blank stares. It will spark our zeal and renew our smile in the hard moments. It will nourish our faith even as we give it away.

PRAYER: A TRANSFORMATIVE ENCOUNTER

The interior life is something God wants to build in us, with our free cooperation. We might think that the decision to pray originates in our own ideas and our own will; but, in fact, the very desire to pray is itself a gift from God. As it was for Adam and Eve; Abraham; Moses; Zechariah and Elizabeth; and, most of all, the young girl who gave her fiat after receiving the message of an angel, so too does God take the initiative with each of us. When we say "yes" to his invitation, the practice of prayer allows us to develop "the habit of being in the presence of the thrice-holy God and in communion with him" (CCC 2565). Prayer acclimates us — helps us to be "at home" — in communion with God.

---

[4] Sherry A. Weddell, *Forming Intentional Disciples: The Path to Knowing and Following Jesus* (Huntington, IN: Our Sunday Visitor, 2012), 151.

It is a preparation for the life of heaven.

How are we to understand the place of prayer in the life of the disciple? What are its essential features? Father Jacques Philippe describes our starting point:

> If the life of prayer is not a technique to be mastered but a grace to be received, a gift from God, then talk about prayer should not focus on describing methods or giving instructions, but on explaining the necessary conditions for receiving the gift. These conditions are certain inner attitudes, certain dispositions of the heart. What ensures progress in the life of prayer, what makes it fruitful, is not so much how we pray as our inner dispositions in beginning and continuing it. Our principal task is to try to acquire, keep, and deepen those dispositions of the heart. God will do the rest.[5]

It is important, then, to identify those conditions of the heart that help a life of prayer to flourish. I would like to suggest three such fundamental dispositions.

1) We must expect prayer to be a real encounter with God.

Many generations of Catholics have grown accustomed to the practice of "saying their prayers" at mealtimes and bedtime. While such a way of conceiving of prayer is helpful without question in developing the discipline of regular prayer, the language employed can be a bit misleading. This is because prayer is not merely something we do. Becoming convicted that prayer

---

[5] Father Jacques Philippe, *Time for God* (Strongsville, OH: Scepter Publishers, 2008), 7.

is an encounter with God moves our interior focus beyond ourselves, to the Other who wants us to truly encounter him.

Of course, we must acknowledge that many Catholics today need to be persuaded that a real encounter with God is actually possible. According to the 2008 Pew Research Center's US Religious Landscape Survey, "only 48% of Catholics were absolutely certain that the God they believed in was a God with whom they could have a personal relationship."[6] For those with little confidence that God can be known personally, such a predisposition impedes their approach to prayer. Because they have no conviction of being able to know and to be known by the Other, the possibility of encounter diminishes. Therefore, when we teach others about prayer, we should not presume that they already believe prayer can be an encounter with God. Or, if they do already have this confidence, they may never have experienced prayer in this way for themselves. Here is where the catechist's actual experience of knowing the presence of God in prayer is invaluable. When we share our lived experience that God is real and able to be encountered, we can nudge a person toward openness.

Through prayer, our students will make the most important discovery of their lives: the sure knowledge of God's presence. We want them to come to experience the kind of prayer that Saint Teresa of Ávila called "contemplation," which she described as "a close sharing between friends; it means taking time frequently to be alone with him who we know loves us."[7] This closeness with our Father in heaven is the essence of the Christian life. It is communion with the One who loves us.

This is why merely saying our prayers while our minds

---

[6] Cited in Weddell, *Forming Intentional Disciples,* 44. The last year that this particular question was asked in the Landscape survey was 2008.

[7] CCC 2709, citing Saint Teresa of Jesus, *The Book of Her Life,* 8, 5 in *The Collected Works of Saint Teresa of Ávila,* trans. Kieran Kavanaugh, OCD, and Otilio Rodriguez, OCD (Washington, DC: Institute of Carmelite Studies, 1976), I, 67.

wander elsewhere — though this is common fare for many of us — is a paltry substitute for the real thing. If we have years of ingrained experience of rote, mindless, mechanical prayer, we can easily miss the enormous potential in this gift God wishes to give us. Each of us must choose to move past previous unhelpful habits of prayer and into the dispositions that lead to encounter and communion. The true and the real in prayer are possible for anyone who attentively seeks.

In this challenge, we might consider the *Catechism's* encouragement: "It is most important that the heart should be present to him to whom we are speaking in prayer" (CCC 2700). Praying from the heart begins with calling to mind our deep and profound need for God, our desire to encounter him. It also involves the constant effort of investing ourselves into our vocal prayers, particularly in times of dryness. Saint Thérèse of Lisieux gives an example of this from her experience of prayer: "Sometimes when my mind is in such great aridity that it is impossible to draw forth one single thought to unite me with God, I very slowly recite an 'Our Father' and then the angelic salutation; then these prayers give me great delight; they nourish my soul much more than if I had recited them precipitately a hundred times."[8] Prayers such as these in times of dryness are important to our spiritual life. They express love and faith in God even when we don't feel his presence. Consequently, they are a clear sign that we love God for himself and not for his consolations. While some might presume that prayer from the heart draws principally on the emotions, "the biblical understanding of 'heart' encompasses much more than emotions; it is the seat of our whole being. At that core (from the Latin, cor, for 'heart'), where we are most aware of our needs, desires, hopes and fears,

---

[8] Thérèse of Lisieux, *The Story of a Soul: The Autobiography of St. Thérèse of Lisieux*, 3rd ed., trans. John Clark, OCD (Washington, DC: ICS Publications, 1996), 243 (MsC 25v).

God comes to meet us."[9]

Blessed Marie Eugene of the Child Jesus, OCD, an extraordinary twentieth-century spiritual writer, describes this encounter in a way that most of us in this age of screens would find challenging: "Prayer is the movement of our whole self, our person, towards God."[10] For us denizens of the twenty-first century, herein lies the difficulty. For a myriad of reasons, we might find ourselves less and less capable of such a full movement of self today. Armed as we are with powerful technology in our pockets that provides endless streams of information and entertainment as well as the promise of immediate connection with others, we should ask ourselves: How do these technologies form our interior life? How do they affect what we think about? How do they impact our capacity to make this movement of the whole self, which is needed for prayer? For authentic prayer requires the encounter of two who are as fully present as possible to one another, just as any meaningful exchange between human beings does. Our attempts at prayer may resemble the person standing at the edge of the water, skipping rocks. Remaining at the water's edge can be a person's experience of prayer through the whole of life. The disciple of Christ, however, engages the water in a different way — getting into the boat, putting out into deep water, and lowering nets for a catch (Lk 5:4).

Consequently, we should note that the idea of prayer as an encounter places demands upon us. In order for a genuine encounter to be possible, we must be alert and present to God in our prayer so that we can move ourselves toward him. And this requires effort, especially today. Pope Emeritus Benedict

---

[9] Elizabeth Siegel, "Part Four: Christian Prayer," in Petroc Willey, Fr. Dominic Scotto, Donald Asci, and Elizabeth Siegel, *A Year with the Catechism: 365 Day Reading Plan* (Huntington, IN: Our Sunday Visitor, 2018), 327 (emphasis author's).

[10] Blessed Marie Eugene of the Child Jesus, *Where the Spirit Breathes: Prayer and Action,* trans. Sr. Mary Thomas Noble, OP, (New York: Alba House, 1988), 53.

XVI puts it this way: "We live in a society in which it seems that every space, every moment must be 'filled' with projects, activities, and noise; there is often no time even to listen or to converse. Dear brothers and sisters, let us not fear to create silence, within and outside ourselves, if we wish to be able not only to become aware of God's voice but also to make out the voice of the person beside us, the voices of others."[11] Most of us know well this battle to prioritize silence, leisure, real connection with others, and to live with technology in a balanced way. One youth minister trenchantly describes the challenges of social media in this way:

> The affirmation and attention that a "like" gives can be a tangible way to fill an ache for communion that is meant to be satisfied by authentic relationships with friends, family, and the Lord. We may regularly complain about the way we see our students turning to social media instead of "real life," yet adults are also vulnerable and can use social media to numb the ache of loneliness that can lead us to call a friend, go on a date, or invest in personal prayer time.[12]

To move our whole selves toward God requires that we seek out silence. For most of us today, this will require that we periodically deny our ingrained inclination to reach for technology to fill moments of silence as they occur. Robert Cardinal Sarah sets before us the way forward, asking, "How can we come to mas-

---

[11] Pope Benedict XVI, "Homily for Eighth Centenary of the Birth of Pope Celestine V," July 4, 2010, in Robert Cardinal Sarah with Nicolas Diat, *The Power of Silence: Against the Dictatorship of Noise*, trans. Michael J. Miller (San Francisco: Ignatius Press, 2017), 27.

[12] Alison Blanchet, "Modern Man Listens More to Witnesses than to Tweeters," *The Catechetical Review* 5, no. 2 (April 2019): 38.

ter our own interior silence? The only answer lies in asceticism, self-renunciation, and humility. If man does not mortify himself, if he stays as he is, he remains outside of God."[13] Time away from screens and devices is more and more a requirement for the Christian serious about developing his life in Christ so that he can live for others. Prayer is a real encounter that requires as complete an investment of ourselves as we can muster.

Let's turn now to a second important disposition for fruitful prayer.

2) We must incline ourselves to both receive and give in prayer.

Above all else, prayer is a personal exchange with God. Prayer is an encounter with God, but it is not just any encounter. Prayer puts us into contact with the God who is love (1 Jn 4:16), who is eternal self-gift. We make our hearts present to God in prayer, because this is the only fitting posture for an encounter with the One who is the very ground of love. Prayer, in its essence, is an exchange of love. For prayer to be this, we must learn two abilities: first, that of attentive receptivity to what God wishes to give; second, we must intentionally make a gift of ourselves to God in how we pray.

Cardinal Sarah highlights the example of Martha and Mary in their encounter with Jesus. While many have interpreted the story as a promotion of the contemplative life (seen in Mary's sitting at the feet of Jesus) over the active (picture Martha's frustrated busyness preparing the meal), Cardinal Sarah points out that what we do for Jesus, what we give to him (Martha) is not to be avoided, but it must be preceded by silence and receptivity to what he wishes to give (Mary). Martha's problem — and sometimes ours as we give to the Lord as catechists — was not that

---

[13] Robert Cardinal Sarah with Nicolas Diat, *The Power of Silence*, 51.

she was preparing the meal, but that she was doing this good work with "an inattentive interior attitude." Jesus then "invites her to stop so as to return to her heart, the place of true welcome and the dwelling place of God's silent tenderness, from which she had been led away by the activity to which she was devoting herself so noisily."[14] This insight is profoundly relevant to every person who seeks God in prayer. For each of us, prayer must first be receptive. We must attune ourselves to what God gives — his grace, his wisdom, his word, his quiet clarity, and, at times, even the feeling of his absence.

As there is a downward movement to prayer, from God to us, so too is there an upward movement.[15] We also give something. And while we give our time, our sacrifices, our worship, and our petitions to the Lord in prayer, the gift that he most desires is the gift of our very selves, a gift that is the very essence of love. Saint Teresa of Ávila writes that, in prayer, "the important thing is not to think much but to love much; and so do that which best stirs you to love. Perhaps we don't know what love is. I wouldn't be very surprised, because it doesn't consist in great delight but in desiring with strong determination to please God in everything."[16] Loving God is ultimately a gift focused toward him rather than being about us. While some think the reason for prayer is self-fulfillment, inner peace, or a deeper joy, the disciple prays first in order to love God. Other fruits may indeed come from prayer, but Christian prayer is ultimately focused away from ourselves, as being for the other as an act of self-giving love.

Blessed Columba Marmion, OSB, also helps us understand

---

[14] Ibid., 27–28.

[15] Jeremy Driscoll, OSB, describes the place of these two movements in the liturgy, and they will be explained more fully in the next chapter. See Jeremy Driscoll, OSB, *What Happens at Mass*, revised edition (Chicago: Liturgy Training Publications, 2011), 10.

[16] Teresa of Jesus, *The Interior Castle*, IV:1 in *The Collected Works of Saint Teresa of Ávila*, trans. Kieran Kavanaugh, OCD, and Otilio Rodriguez, OCD (Washington, DC: Institute of Carmelite Studies, 1980), II, 319.

the gift we give to God in prayer. For Marmion, prayer is a "conversation of a child of God with its Heavenly Father, to adore him, to praise him, to say 'I love you' to him, to learn to know his will and to obtain from him the help that is necessary to do that will."[17] In other words, no matter the particular form our prayer takes, the praying person is Other-focused, directing mind, heart, and will in a posture of self-giving toward God. Most important is that we gather together our gift of self — in our aspirations, words, postures, sacrifices — as an upward gift. We must join ourselves to our words and gestures, so that they truly represent us. The more we are able to pray from our hearts in this way, the more our prayer takes on the quality of a gift. This kind of prayer opens up great potential within us as we seek union with God.

3) Finally, we must expect to be changed through prayer.

Such a loving exchange is meant to transform us, to conform us more and more to the One who is our model of holiness and charity.

I won't forget the April day when I was getting ready to leave my apartment to take an exam for which I did not feel adequately prepared. As I was hurrying around, gathering my things, I asked my wife to pray for me, because I felt I needed a miracle to be able to do well. As I was opening the door to leave for the university, the phone rang, and the call was for me. I picked up the receiver and was stunned to hear my professor's voice on the other end of the line, informing me that because of the serious winter storm that had just hit, the exam was canceled; instead, students were to turn in a paper. I had barely noticed the snow that was steadily coming down, particularly because in my experience of living in the Midwest, it never snowed much in late

---

[17] Blessed Columba Marmion, *Christ the Life of the Soul* (Bethesda, MD: Zaccheus Press, 2005), 417.

April. What joy and relief I felt with such an immediate response to my wife's (clearly very powerful) prayers!

How many times do we approach the Lord in prayer, asking him to change something — a person, a bad habit, a feared outcome, or some difficult circumstance? Prayers such as these are important, and the Lord himself encourages frequent and persistent prayers of petition (e.g., Mt 7:7; Mt 6:28–34; Jn 14:13). But our prayers regarding some difficulty God has allowed in our life never change God's mind. His intent with these prayers is quite different: He wants our experience of prayer to change us. And if we are able, even just sometimes, to enter into the receiving and giving of love through prayer, we cannot avoid being changed.

Through prayer, our intentions and desires are purified, healed, elevated, and conformed to the divine will. Experienced catechist Elizabeth Siegel explains:

> When we think God does not hear our prayers, our faith is being tested. God wants our relationship with him to be authentic, and not based solely on our desire to get something from him. If we are willing, he purifies us from this selfish love towards a love of God simply for who he is. ... The fact that our prayer does not go the way we intend does not mean that God is absent. God is always at work in our sincere prayer, he is always seeking our good, he is always bringing us to salvation, and he is always preparing us to receive the riches he has for us.[18]

Christian prayer, then, is a personal encounter with God. As

---

[18] Elizabeth Siegel, "Part Four: Christian Prayer," in Petroc Willey et al., *A Year with the Catechism*, 355.

we receive and give, we enter into a divine way of loving. And immersion in the life of God is meant to change us, to sanctify us, to make us gradually more like the One whom we follow as disciples.

PRAYER: PRACTICAL CONSIDERATIONS FOR THE CATECHIST

Our life of prayer is meant to create within us a deep reservoir of living water. This overflowing water then sustains us in our own life with Christ and in our work as catechists. It is important to note that prayer does not always remove difficulties; rather, it is how we cling to God, particularly in our weakness and in the face of difficulties.

Teresa Hawes from Vermont is a professed member of the Notre Dame de Vie secular institute initially founded in France. As a member of this institute, in addition to the vows of poverty, chastity, and obedience, Teresa has made the additional commitment to spend two hours in silent prayer each day, allowing her apostolate of teaching to flow out of her life with God. Teresa shares an experience she had of allowing prayer to be the source for her catechetical work:

> One Saturday morning I was preparing to lead a prayer group that evening. The Bible, the *Catechism*, other reference books and notes were spread out before me. I don't remember the specific topic, but I do remember that I had been carrying it in daily prayer for quite some time, trying to knit together a teaching that would nourish the avid souls in this group. That morning, nothing seemed to fit anywhere, and I was overcome with utter helplessness. The meeting was only a few hours away, and I

felt completely incompetent and at a loss, unable to say anything good, true, or beautiful. I even called the priest who mentored this group, telling him he would have to teach that evening as I was useless. He laughed at me, said some encouraging words and hung up. There I was amidst my mess of books and papers — all I could do was close my eyes and ask Mother Mary to help me surrender everything to Our Lord. After some quiet time in prayer, I took up the thread of the talk again; a way to sort out the messy knot of references and thoughts started to become clear. The "peace surpassing all understanding" settled into my heart, and the talk did turn out well.

Since then, a similar experience of powerlessness has become my usual lot at some point prior to any catechetical lesson or presentation. I recognize and welcome it now as a good sign: The Holy Spirit wants me to get out of the way, detaching myself from my preparation, trusting him to take the reins. "Without me you can do nothing," Jesus taught. Yet, he also commissioned us to be his witnesses even to the ends of the earth. How is that possible? I remember that Therese of the Child Jesus found an answer when she was asked to teach the novices, trusting Jesus to give her what they needed. She also shared that inspiration did not come during her two hours of silent prayer, but afterward, as she journeyed through daily life. That has been my little experience, too: The Holy Spirit uses the receptive qualities that are given to us in our baptismal grace [cf. CCC 1830] to intervene directly in our prayer and in our action in the midst of our ordinary, daily lives. We often feel the opposite of the grace we are receiving,[19] which explains my impression of utter helplessness. Plus, prideful as I am, I probably would not have the humility to get out of the way, trust, and surrender if I was not backed into a corner by this experience of weakness. Praised be Jesus who awaits my act of faith, strengthened in prayer, to use me as his instrument, as he wills.

Wherever we are now in our commitment to prayer, there is always room to grow. As we conclude this chapter, let's consider five simple ways we can deepen the reservoir from which we draw our spiritual nourishment as catechists.

1) Turn up the silence.

A first step is simply to introduce more silence into daily life. Exterior silence creates the capacity for interior silence, which is the prerequisite for real prayer. Cardinal Sarah writes:

No prophet ever encountered God without withdrawing into solitude and silence. Moses, Elijah, and John the Baptist encountered God in the great silence of the desert. Today, too, monks seek God in solitude and silence. I am speaking, not just about a geographical solitude or movement, but about an interior state. It is

---

[19] Marie-Eugene of the Child Jesus, OCD, *I Want to See God: A Practical Synthesis of Carmelite Spirituality*, vol. 1, trans. Sr. M. Verda Clare, CSC (Notre Dame, IN: Fides Publishers, 1953), 338–60. See especially 353–54, where Blessed Marie-Eugene explains this negative experience and why it is the most constant and authentic sign of God's action.

not enough to be quiet, either. It is necessary
to become silence. For, even before the desert,
the solitude, and the silence, God is already in
man. The true desert is within us, in our soul.
Strengthened with this knowledge, we can understand how silence is indispensable if we are
to find God. The Father waits for his children in
their own hearts.[20]

So, take a quiet walk every day. Spend time in silence before Jesus in the Blessed Sacrament. Turn off the music or the podcast
on your commute to work. Arrive ten minutes early to Mass. Sit
quietly before going to bed. Taking steps toward God in silence
will increase our capacities for prayer.

2) Identify naturally recurring opportunities for prayer, which will help prayer become a regular (and difficult-to-forget) habit.

I was recently struck by the habit of someone who described how
important it has been for him to make room on his bedside table
for a crucifix. Every morning when he first wakes, he reaches for
the crucifix, so that his first conscious movement of the day is
to raise his mind and heart to God rather than reaching for his
iPhone to check messages.

I started off fatherhood convinced of my responsibility to
pray for my children. Yet, I had a hard time remembering to
do so with any real consistency. An idea learned in observing
another family has been valuable for me. As I had seen them do,
I trace the sign of the cross on our children's foreheads as part
of our bedtime ritual. Over the years, that simple habit of blessing has developed into a time of silent prayer over each of the

---

[20] Robert Cardinal Sarah with Nicolas Diat, *The Power of Silence*, 23.

girls every night. They're used to it. I'm used to it. And it's a way for me, without fail, to pray for each of them individually every night. My friend Sean prays a Rosary every day, and years ago he started praying it for one of his family members each day of the week. Thanks to this ritual, it has become automatic to pray specifically for one family member each day. My wife used to pray Hail Marys for her elementary school students as they filed into the room before each class. It was a great source of peace and strength for her teaching. When prayer becomes a habit, we become intentional and consistent, thereby bringing infinite good into our lives and those of the people we lift up in this way.

As catechists, we might ask ourselves: Where are the natural hook moments in our daily routine that can help us intercede more consistently for those we teach? Perhaps we can develop the habit of praying for them as we drive to and from our meeting place, or at the beginning of our lesson-planning time, or before the tabernacle upon our arrival at the church. A public school teacher who is a Christian once described how he would arrive early to school each day and sit in the desks of each of his students, quietly praying for each one's needs before they arrived to school.

Find those recurring moments in daily life that can be intentionally dedicated to prayer. By forming these habits, praying for those entrusted to us for catechesis becomes a consistent practice, even amidst the busyness of life. Praying regularly on behalf of our students will increase the possibilities for grace to move in them inside and outside the classroom. It will also help us into an authentic way of generous love for those we teach.

3) Pray with Scripture.

As our specific mission revolves around the proclamation and teaching of the word of God, Scripture ought to occupy an important position in our personal prayer. Reading and praying with God's word is a way to meet the Lord and to immerse ourselves in his way of seeing, thinking, and living.

In the catechist's spiritual life, there is no substitute for soaking in the content of the Gospels. Our reading of these texts, however, should not be undertaken in the usual ways we read books. Many saints through the centuries have shown how to read Scripture in ways aligned with its nature as Divine Revelation: by allowing it to lead us to silence, to deep reflection, to a responsiveness to what we read, and to a commitment to conform ourselves to the One who speaks to us through the text.

These important elements are each seen in *lectio divina*, a particularly profound way of pondering the Scriptures. Lectio divina (literally, "divine reading") is an ancient monastic practice of prayerfully reading Scripture in such a way that we seek to encounter God. Rather than reading many passages at a time, when we do lectio divina we instead engage a shorter selection, seeking to truly "take in" the Scripture, attentive and responsive to what God is saying to us personally. The passage is prayerfully read three or four times — each time with a distinct intention — so that we might focus ourselves on the text. First, we read the passage aloud (*lectio*), slowly and reverently, attentive to particular words or phrases that the Holy Spirit brings to our attention. We might consider reading it again silently with the same observant disposition. Next, we meditate on the passage (*meditatio*) and, in particular, those words that were brought to mind. The objective here is to spend time pondering, prayerfully engaging the particular words and phrases that caught our attention, working to take God's word to heart. The last step is to make a prayerful, personal response to God for what has been received in the time of prayer (*oratio*). We might consider writing down what especially struck us in our reflection. We respond here to God with words of gratitude and praise, or perhaps with questions that have arisen in our prayer, or a petition for healing, or a specific resolution for change.

A special grace can be received as a gift from God during our time of prayer — that of contemplation (*contemplatio*). This is the serene experience of just being with God, resting in his loving presence. As my friend and colleague Deacon Stephen Miletic, PhD, describes it, "There is an overwhelming awareness that, for example, every molecule in the room is replete with the Divine Presence, an experience of great and deep peace that is seemingly 'uncaused' by anything we do or have done. One does not arrive at contemplation from doing steps 1 to 3 properly, from fasting, ascetical practices, etc. It arrives when God deems it necessary to assist us in this way."

Another scriptural discipline that can sustain us is reading and praying in advance with the Sunday Mass readings. Not only will we come to know God's word more deeply, but this practice also prepares us to more actively and consciously receive God's word as it is proclaimed in the liturgy.

4) Pray in a way that strengthens the connection between faith and life.

The 1993 "Guide for Catechists" suggests that the prayer of catechists should lead to a "coherence and authenticity of life." A catechist's prayer life should involve "their whole being. Before they preach the word, they must make it their own and live by it."[21] Therefore, the prayer of a catechist should not be a purely ethereal exercise that is not related to life. Prayer is important to integrating the Faith in how we live, sanctifying every aspect of our experience. This is, of course, especially important for those who form others in the Christian life.

For instance, ending each day with an examination of conscience is essential to making progress in holiness of life, keeping

---

[21] Congregation for the Evangelization of Peoples, "Guide for Catechists," Vatican.va, art. 8.

us attuned to our need for God's mercy. In his classic book, *Introduction to the Devout Life*, Saint Francis de Sales recommends four steps to this examination:

1. We give thanks to God for having kept us during the past day.
2. We examine how we conducted ourselves throughout the whole course of the day. To do so more easily, we may reflect on where, with whom, and in what work we have been engaged.
3. If we find that we have done any good, we must thank God for it. On the other hand, if we have done anything wrong in thought, word, or deed, we must ask pardon of his Divine Majesty with a resolution to confess it at the first opportunity and to make careful amendment for it.
4. After this, we recommend to God's providence our body and soul, the Church, our relatives, and friends. We beg our Lady, our guardian angel, and the saints to watch over us and for us.[22]

Regularly examining ourselves deepens our personal conversion, helping us to grow in faith, hope, and charity, which transforms our disposition toward God and other people.

We can exercise our baptismal priesthood when we offer up our experiences in life as loving, sacrificial gifts to God. This practice sanctifies the whole of daily life — our struggles in suffering and little defeats, but also our joys and our victories. The Church tells us that every experience of ordinary life is worthy of being offered out of love to God: "For all their works, prayers

---

[22] Saint Francis de Sales, *Introduction to the Devout Life*, trans. John K. Ryan (New York: Doubleday, 1989), 95–96.

and apostolic endeavors, their ordinary married and family life, their daily occupations, their physical and mental relaxation, if carried out in the Spirit, and even the hardships of life, if patiently borne — all these become 'spiritual sacrifices acceptable to God through Jesus Christ' [1 Pt 2:5]. Together with the offering of the Lord's body, they are most fittingly offered in the celebration of the Eucharist" (*Lumen Gentium,* 34).

Giving every aspect of life as a sacrifice to God in love (to include our physical and mental relaxation) is the way of divine love and is our priestly work for the sanctification of the world.

6) Pray while you teach.

I was always taken aback by one of my theology professors, who used to teach with rosary beads in his hand. Watching closely, I soon realized that his fingers were slowly moving from bead to bead as he taught. While such an ability to do two complex things at the same time eludes me, I do intentionally follow the advice of Saint Teresa of Calcutta on how to pray in daily life. She wrote, "You can pray while you work. Work doesn't stop prayer and prayer doesn't stop work. It requires only that small raising of the mind to him: 'I love you God, I trust you, I believe in you, I need you now.' Small things like that. They are wonderful prayers."[23] I have found this way of prayer so practically helpful: Through the ebbs and flows of teaching, short darts of the heart toward the Lord keep me oriented to him and open to his inspirations: "Be with us, Lord! Give me the words! Help us respond to you! Wake up that kid in the back row!"

I have also known teachers who, when studying a particularly challenging teaching or seemingly incredible account from the Gospels, stop teaching to turn to God with the students.

---

[23] Mother Teresa, quoted in Jaya Chalika and Edward Le Joly, eds., *The Joy in Loving: A Guide to Daily Living* (New York: Penguin Books, 1997), 73.

"Lord, this is hard to grasp. We know we are standing before a great mystery here. Open our eyes to your way of seeing!" Such a "prayer break" can make a strong impression on participants, teaching them the quintessential posture of the disciple before the mysteries contained in Scripture.

Prayer is both our lifeline and our reservoir. It is a life of intimate communion with God, who loves us infinitely. A commitment to prayer not only brings us into the life and love of God, but it also empowers our teaching and our conversations with those we teach. We simply cannot do without it and hope to be fruitful in our work for the Lord.

CHAPTER THREE

The Catechist *in Christ*
Living and Teaching from
the Sacramental Encounter

We are made for communion: first with God, and then with one another. Our hearts are uneasy and unsatisfied apart from such communion. This "restlessness" (as Saint Augustine called it) is intended to draw us more and more out of ourselves and deeper into the life of divine love for which we were created. In the previous chapter, we considered the importance of prayer in our life with God, and its significance also in our catechesis. Prayer allows us, as individuals, both to love God and to receive his love and grace by spending time in his presence. And prayer makes us credible witnesses as we teach the Faith and live for others.

In this chapter, we turn to the unique position of the sacraments in the life of the catechist. Our students ask challenging sacramental questions: Do the sacraments really matter? Do they actually do anything? We can best answer their questions when our teaching is illumined by our own intentional sacramental life.

Saint John Paul II once wrote: "It is in the sacraments, especially in the Eucharist, that Christ Jesus works in fullness for the transformation of human beings."[1] This conviction, above all others, must stand unobstructed in the way the catechist lives. The sacraments are a uniquely transformative place of divine encounter. Established by Christ himself, they effect what they signify, making present the mysterious reality to which they point. The waters of baptism, for instance, bring about within us a real death to the domination of sin and a new life in the light of Christ and in the family of God.[2] The outpouring of the Holy Spirit through the nuptial blessing in the Sacrament of Matrimony gives husband and wife divine capacities for love and fidelity, a potential for a supernatural way of loving that did not exist in their relationship before receiving the sacrament (CCC 1638–42). And holy Communion brings about (you guessed it!) a holy communion, deepening our supernatural friendship with God in ways that meet our heart's desire and send us renewed into the world (CCC 1391–1401).

Sacred Scripture and Sacred Tradition provide us what we need if we are to understand the true power of the sacraments. However, we must soberly acknowledge that there are serious challenges today in how our Catholic teaching regarding the

---

[1] Saint John Paul II, *Catechesi Tradendae*, accessed April 20, 2020, Vatican.va, par. 23.
[2] See especially *Catechism of the Catholic Church*, 1262–74.

sacraments is believed and lived.

SACRAMENTAL FAITH: SIGNS OF HOPE AND CRISIS

In the opening chapters of Victor Hugo's *Les Misérables,* we meet an extraordinary man: the saintly bishop. Full of charity, he is well known even beyond his diocese for his humility and holiness. When the paroled convict Jean Valjean knocks roughly on his door, the bishop welcomes him inside. Valjean has already been refused admittance to the local inns and the homes of several Christian families. He has even been savagely chased by a dog out of its kennel where he had hoped to sleep. Jean Valjean is stupefied as the bishop invites him inside to eat and offers him a place in his own home for the night. Valjean bluntly declares his identity, showing the bishop his paperwork identifying him as a paroled convict. The bishop smiles and says to him: "This is not my house; it is the house of Jesus Christ. This door does not demand of him who enters whether he has a name, but whether he has a grief. You suffer, you are hungry and thirsty; you are welcome. And do not thank me; do not say that I receive you in my house. No one is at home here, except the man who needs a refuge. I say to you, who are passing by, that you are much more at home here than I am myself. Everything here is yours."[3]

The bishop's generous charity, seen especially after Jean Valjean later attacks him and steals from him, turns the paroled convict's world upside down. The book tells of the astonishing impact that this destitute man's encounter with the bishop has, not just on Valjean, but on many others. Encountering Christ in the bishop indeed makes Jean Valjean a new man. Hugo's story reveals the effects that the Church can have on the world when bishops become saints, and when Catholics live true to what

---

[3] Victor Hugo, *Les Misérables* (San Diego, CA: Canterbury Classics, 2012), 71–72.

they receive in the sacraments.

While the bishop is a fictionalized character, we need not look too extensively into the lives of the saints to find real-life witnesses to the transformational power of the sacraments. What are we to make of Blessed Imelda Lambertini, who purportedly died of joy upon receiving her first holy Communion? Or Saint Thomas Aquinas, who wrote of the Eucharist, "O precious and wonderful banquet that brings us salvation and contains all sweetness! Could anything be of more intrinsic value?"[4] What about Saint Thomas More, who began each day with quiet prayer, study, and Mass? This continual immersion in prayer and in the liturgy so conformed him to Christ over the course of his life, that he was able to write these resplendent words in the margins of his prayer book while awaiting his execution:

> Give me Thy grace, good Lord
> To set the world at naught;
> To set my mind fast upon Thee,
> And not to hang upon the blast of men's mouths ... [5]

If we seek a present-day example, Chiara Corbella Petrillo's witness to the transformative power of the sacraments is remarkable. By the grace of the sacraments, Chiara and her husband, Enrico, cultivated a beautiful married life, finding great peace in God even as they lost their first two children within thirty minutes of each one's respective birth. Hopeful and pregnant a third time, Chiara received the devastating news that her body was being silently ravaged by cancer. Facing intense skepticism from her doctors, Chiara refused cancer treatment, as it would endanger the life of their child. Her peace and joy, rooted deeply

---

[4] Feast of Corpus Christi, cited in *Liturgy of the Hours*, Vol. III, 610.
[5] Gerard B. Wegemer, *Thomas More: A Portrait of Courage* (Princeton, NJ: Scepter Publishers, 1995), 191.

in her encounter with Christ in the sacraments, is a stirring testimony. She died in 2012 at the age of twenty-eight.

In a note written to her toddler son while she lay dying in a hospital, Chiara wrote: "For the little I have understood during these years, I can tell you only that Love is the center of our life. Because we are born from an act of love, we live in order to love and in order to be loved, and we die in order to know the true love of God. The goal of our life is to love and to be always ready to learn how to love others as only God is able to teach you."[6]

How is such extraordinary joy and charity possible? The disciple of Jesus knows that these are the fruits we should expect as we draw closer to God in the sacraments.

While there are many signs of sacramental fruitfulness in the saints and in shining exemplars among us today, we also know that we are sadly besieged by many counter-signs. We live today in a time of scandal in our Church — and often these scandals are not just moral in nature. They also have an unfortunate sacramental dimension.

For example, we are all too familiar these days with countersigns of the Sacrament of Holy Orders in the lives of some priests and bishops. In the Sacrament of Holy Orders, a principal effect of the sacrament is that "the recipient is configured to Christ by a special grace of the Holy Spirit, so that he may serve as Christ's instrument" (cf. CCC 1581–89). If a priest or bishop lives a double life, we can have confidence that he continues objectively to be Christ's instrument in making the grace and the effects of the sacraments available to us.[7] However, the personal union and configuration to Christ intended by God for the priest or bishop

---

[6] Simone Troisi and Cristiana Paccini, *Chiara Corbella Petrillo: A Witness to Joy*, trans. Charlotte J. Fasi (Manchester, NH: Sophia Institute Press, 2015), 158. In 2017, Chiara's cause for sainthood was opened.

[7] The *Catechism of the Catholic Church* is very helpful on this point, stating that "from the moment that a sacrament is celebrated in accordance with the intention of the Church, the power of Christ and his Spirit acts in and through it, independently of the personal holiness of the minister" (CCC 1128).

is obstructed.

The Second Vatican Council describes the possibility, should a person (whether a member of the clergy, a religious community, or a layperson) not cooperate with grace, of receiving a sacrament in vain.[8] What happens when we receive the sacraments without cooperating with their specific graces? It doesn't take long before the dissonance between what we receive and how we live causes a loss of faith in the sacraments — for ourselves certainly, but also for those around us. Thus, our confidence in the reality of sacramental grace can be diminished when we see the sacramentally married living unfaithfully or in deep division; the newly confirmed immediately abandoning sacramental practice; and the baptized failing to become missionary disciples of the One with whom they are intimately joined by baptismal grace. Immersed in a culture of these sacramental counter-signs, many today now have no expectations of the sacraments. Some tragically conclude that the sacraments are, in essence, pious superstitions, empty ceremonies that affect nothing. For them, the sacraments are merely human rites of passage, rather than transforming encounters with God that conform us more closely to Christ who is our Life. Moreover, because the sacramental life lacks the strong familial and cultural supports of previous generations, it is easily abandoned.

Therefore, our great need today (along with clear and faithful teaching) is for authentic witnesses to the fruitfulness of the sacraments. We need concrete examples of real people who live lives of radical love flowing from the sacramental encounter. We need an army of disciples — married, single, children, teenagers, religious, priests, bishops, and catechists — who consciously and intentionally draw upon the grace of the sacraments to live lives of substantial, self-sacrificing love.

---

[8] Second Vatican Council, *Sacrosanctum Concilium*, accessed April 20, 2020, Vatican.va, par. 11.

THE DYNAMISM OF THE SACRAMENTS

Here is perhaps the pivotal question: How are we to understand the movement and the demands of sacramental grace within us?

Perhaps the most helpful image was given in that most solemn hour between the Last Supper and Jesus' fervent prayer in the Garden of Gethsemane. It was in these moments — at the very apex of his time with his disciples — that Jesus speaks to them of the unimaginable intimacy that disciples are to enjoy with their Creator. After giving his disciples his Body and Blood at the Last Supper, bringing into being a deep and real communion with them, the Lord turns to his disciples and says: "I am the vine, you are the branches. Whoever remains in me and I in him will bear much fruit, because without me you can do nothing" (Jn 15:5).

The Lord makes clear here that his relationship with his disciples would not merely be that of Creator to creature, Teacher to student, or even Friend to friend. While each of these kinds of relationships, by grace, remains, the baptized Christian enters into a mysterious union with Christ — and through him with our Father in the power of the Holy Spirit. The image Christ uses is an agricultural one that would have been familiar to his disciples: branches grafted to vines. Christ's will for them (and for every person wishing to follow him) is that they be united to him just as a branch is grafted to the vine, becoming one and the same thing. This union is effected in the Sacrament of Baptism and is strengthened and nourished through each of the sacraments in distinctive ways.

The new relationship that the disciple enjoys with Christ, then, is a relationship of intimate union. If we consider this — and dwell on the sheer magnitude of what we become through Christ in the sacraments — the image of Vine and branches is as shocking as it is beautiful. How valuable and precious every human being is to him! In heaven, the Lord won't drop in on us every couple of weeks to make sure we're comfortable. We were created for union. It is a union that takes us up wondrously into the life and love of the Most Blessed Trinity. Liturgical theologian Jean Corbon describes this life within the Trinity, as well as what it demands of us, with particular vividness:

> Yes, the mysterious river of divine communion is an outpouring of love among the Three, and in it eternal life consists. Each person is gift and acceptance of gift, never varying yet not motionless; each is an élan that is enamored of the Other but in pure transparency; each is joy given gratuitously and accepted freely. To this communion with its ebb and flow, to this rhythm of love from which love overflows, no living being can draw near unless the veil of mortality is rent asunder. The human heart cannot contain this inexpressible joy as long as the last attachment to "self" has not been severed.[9]

While we were made for this union in love with God, this relationship with God also puts us into a family relationship with every person who has entered and remained in this life in Christ. We can scarcely begin to imagine the goodness and beauty of being in this family! Saint John of the Cross, when contemplating this mystery of all that the soul receives in God, exclaims: "Mine are the heavens and mine is the earth. ... The angels are mine, and the Mother of God, and all things are mine; and God himself is mine and for me, because Christ is mine and all for me. What do you ask, then, and seek, my soul? Yours is all of this, and all is for you. Do not engage yourself in something less or pay heed to

---

[9] Jean Corbon, *The Wellspring of Worship*, trans. Matthew J. O'Connell (Mahwah, NJ: Paulist Press, 1988), 16.

the crumbs that fall from your Father's table. Go forth and exult in your glory! Hide yourself in it and rejoice!"[10] The follower of Jesus, then, is not merely one who accepts his teaching. The Christian life is not only about what we do. The disciple lives from a position of encounter, intimate closeness, with Divine Love himself — and with all who are in Love's family.

Moreover, God expects fruit from the vine. "I am the true vine, and my Father is the vine grower. He takes away every branch in me that does not bear fruit, and every one that does he prunes so that it bears more fruit" (Jn 15:1–2). We gain a vivid picture here of the great dynamism of the Christian life. Being grafted to the vine is what makes fruitfulness possible. Encounter, grace, union — each is given as a great gift so that spiritual fruit would be tangibly born in the life of each disciple. In fact, fruitfulness is the whole point of the Christian life. This is why we can only follow the supernatural teaching of Jesus when we are connected to him. Indeed, living as a disciple becomes possible only as the divine life flows through us, as sap flows from the vine into the branches.

There is, then, a great consequence to this life of union with God. Living a sacramental life — cooperating with God's gift of grace — will require us to move outside of ourselves in charity and service to the world, especially to those most in need. Each of us will one day be asked, "What did you do with this great gift of communion with me?"

THE CATECHIST: LIVING FROM THE SACRAMENTAL ENCOUNTER

How can we live sacramentally, conformed more and more to the way of divine love? Let's consider five ways forward.

---

[10] Saint John of the Cross, *The Collected Works of Saint John of the Cross*, trans. Kieran Kavanaugh, OCD, and Otilio Rodriguez, OCD (Washington, DC: ICS Publications, 1991), 87–88.

1) Avoid the tendency toward minimalism. Instead, generously invest in sacramental living.

Previous generations of Catholics were familiar with what we call "the precepts of the Church."[11] Recall a few of them with me: As Catholics, we are required:

- to attend Mass on Sundays and holy days of obligation;
- to go to confession and receive holy Communion once a year;
- to fast and abstain from eating meat on the days prescribed by the Church.

These positive laws represent the basics of sacramental participation necessary to a Catholic life. At a minimum, today's catechists must meet these standards. Unfortunately, it is possible here to fall into a minimalist living of the Christian life. How late can I arrive at Mass (or how early can I leave) and still meet my Sunday obligation? Do I have to confess every sin? How many Church teachings may I disagree with and yet still finish RCIA and be baptized (thereby pleasing my fiancée so we can be married in the Church)? Many of us at some point have asked questions such as these. But growing to become a disciple opens up new vistas because the Christian life is a generous life, in what we give to God and in what we offer to others.

As disciples, we want to generously live out our sacramental life. Perhaps we can take intentional steps to cultivate interior silence before Mass, so we are focused and ready to invest ourselves in the "summit" and "font" of the whole Christian life.[12] We can celebrate our baptismal anniversaries with gusto or spend

---

[11] For a full list, see CCC 2041–43.

12 Second Vatican Council, *Sacrosanctum Concilium*, accessed April 20, 2020, Vatican.va, par. 10.

special time in prayer with our spouse on wedding anniversaries, alert to the deepening of conversion brought about through matrimonial grace within the past year. Investing in our sacramental life testifies to those around us that sacramental living is a priority for us. But this witness for others is secondary in importance. Catechetical leader and writer Bill Keimig points out just how important it is that the sacraments become a place of true nourishment for us. God wants us to come to depend upon the sacraments. Keimig writes, "Liturgy must be need-based. In your own faith life the liturgy must be an uncompromising and unequivocal need of your soul, so that you could say, 'I need the liturgy! I need what it offers on a daily basis. I can't imagine life without it.'"[13]

2) Join yourself to the actions of Christ the Priest.

Perhaps you've heard the questions, "Why do I have to go to Mass every Sunday? Can't I just pray on my own?" We can answer this only by first responding to a related question: Is there any real difference between liturgical and personal prayer?

Most catechist-disciples would emphatically respond, "The Eucharist!" And this is true and essential to our answer. There is also a broader answer that, when understood, makes a great difference in how we approach the liturgy.

The Mass is not personal prayer. It is not even the gathered personal prayers of a congregation of individuals. It is a qualitatively different experience, for the liturgy is the prayer of the Mystical Body of Jesus Christ. Christ, the Head of the Body, prays the Sacred Liturgy, allowing the members of his Body (you and me) to join ourselves through the working of the Holy Spirit to this great prayer of Christ.

---

[13] William Keimig, "Liturgical Catechesis in the RCIA Process," in James C. Pauley, *Liturgical Catechesis in the 21ˢᵗ Century: A School of Discipleship* (Chicago: Liturgy Training Publications, 2017), 200.

But to whom does Christ pray? If we listen carefully to the language of the liturgy, we will have our answer. For instance, consider the words of the doxology: "Through him and with him and in him, O God Almighty Father, in the unity of the Holy Spirit, all glory and honor are yours!" We see here the Trinitarian nature and direction of the Mass: The Holy Spirit joins us all (with our cooperation) to Christ, who is the Head of his Body, and in unity we join him in his priestly offering to the Father. This great prayer of the liturgy is not ours, but it is Christ's. And we have the great privilege to join in his liturgical work, offering praise to our Father in heaven and interceding for the sanctification of the world.

If we don't grasp this way of seeing inherent to the liturgy, we miss what is most essential. We don't actually pray to Jesus at Mass. But we do encounter him, and this encounter is like none other. We are joined to him in the intimate unity of his prayer to his Father. And in the liturgy, his mission becomes ours, united as we are in his Mystical Body. Christ Jesus re-presents his saving sacrifice on Calvary to his Father, as the act that gives maximum glory to God and maximum grace to the world, and we have the great honor of joining him in his priestly offering.

Personal prayer and the corporate prayer (from the Latin *corpus*, meaning "body") of the liturgy are, as we can see, quite distinctive from one another. Yet, both are necessary to a flourishing Catholic life. Knowing that we pray in union with Christ, in adoration of the Father, for the great good of the world will open us to the true meaning of our participation in the sacred liturgy.

3) Invest in the liturgy's twofold movement of love.
God wants to draw us into his dynamic giving and receiving of divine love. Lifted up by the Holy Spirit into the unity of the Mystical Body of Christ, when we are present at Mass, we partic-

ipate in Christ's own offering to the Father. In a compelling passage, the *Catechism* states: "God himself is an eternal exchange of love, Father, Son and Holy Spirit, and he has destined us to share in that exchange" (221). Immersion into this divine exchange of love is possible in the liturgy like nowhere else, joined as we are to Christ as members of his body.

University of Notre Dame theologian David Fagerberg puts it this way: In the liturgy, "the Trinity's circulation of love turns itself outward, and in humility the Son and Spirit work the Father's good pleasure for all creation, which is to invite our ascent to participate in the very life of God; however, this cannot be forced, it must be done with our cooperation."[14] The implications of this are astounding. What is perhaps most important is that we see the essential dynamic of liturgical prayer. There is, for us, both a receiving and a giving. There is what Father Jeremy Driscoll, OSB, calls, a "downwards" and an "upwards movement" to liturgical prayer. "The first is a movement from God the Father to the world, while the second is a movement from the world to God the Father."[15]

The downward sacramental motion is a movement of sanctification, through which our Father gives to us through his Son in the Holy Spirit. To name just a few of the extraordinary gifts he gives us in this way, he gives us new life, freedom from original sin, and adoption into his family in baptism; he additionally offers us forgiveness and healing in sacramental confession; and he gives us Christ Jesus in word and sacrament in the Mass. Each sacrament is like this: God gives of himself, and that gift lifts us up into his divine life and love.

We call the upward movement of liturgical prayer worship

---

[14] David W. Fagerberg, *On Liturgical Asceticism* (Washington, DC: Catholic University of America Press, 2013), 9.

[15] Jeremy Driscoll, OSB, *What Happens at Mass,* revised edition (Chicago: Liturgy Training Publications, 2011), 10.

or adoration. In private prayer, we may have had many experiences of praise and adoration of God. But in Mass, remembering that we are joined to Christ in his prayer to the Father, this movement of adoration and praise is going to be different from our experiences in personal prayer. If we want to understand this upward liturgical movement, we must come to see the very particular way Christ adores the Father through his sacred liturgy. Because, joined to Jesus, his act of adoration becomes our own. Within the liturgy, this will be our primary way of loving God.

Jesus loves the Father by lifting up before the eyes of the Father his loving and obedient self-sacrifice on Calvary. We learn from Sacred Scripture and from the *Catechism*: "Jesus Christ, the one priest of the new and eternal Covenant, 'entered, not into a sanctuary made by human hands ... but into heaven itself, now to appear in the presence of God on our behalf' (Heb 9:24). There Christ permanently exercises his priesthood, for he 'always lives to make intercession' for 'those who draw near to God through him' (Heb 7:25). As 'high priest of the good things to come' (Heb 9:11) he is the center and the principal actor of the liturgy that honors the Father in heaven" (662).

We worship the Father at Mass in joining the priest-presider, who stands in the person of Christ, the Head of the Body, offering to the Father the saving sacrifice of his Son on the Cross. How unimaginably good it is that Christ Jesus invites us into this movement of love toward his Father!

Blessed Columba Marmion, OSB, helps us rightly understand this upward movement, in relation to this re-presentation of the Paschal Mystery to the Father within the Mass. Considering all that God gives us in the liturgy, Marmion writes: "We owe to God, in return, a more than ordinary thanksgiving for this ineffable gift. What shall we give to God that will be worthy of him? His son Jesus. In offering his Son to him, we give back to him the gift he has given to us ... and no gift could be more pleasing to him. ... Let us then, along with the priest, offer the Holy Sacrifice. Let us offer to the Eternal Father his Divine Son after having received him at the holy banquet."[16]

But then, there is an interesting twist. We participate in the re-presentation of the Paschal Mystery by interiorly joining the presider as he lifts the Son up to his Father — but this fundamental movement opens within us another offering we can make to the Father. Marmion writes, "But let us, through love, also offer ourselves with him, that we may in everything do what his divine will shows us we should do. This is the most perfect present we could give to God."[17] Swimming in the waters of divine, self-giving generosity, it is only fitting that with the offering of the Paschal Victim, we also offer ourselves in love to the Father. And there is no aspect of our life and experience that is not, through Christ, worthy of being lifted up to our heavenly Father as a free gift.

What happens, then, when God pours himself out entirely in a gift to us, and we make of ourselves a gift to him, offered along with the sacrifice of Jesus? This is a foretaste and a very real participation in the eternal exchange of love that is the life of God. Through the grace of God and the atmosphere of supremely generous love within the sacred liturgy, we are brought into communion with the Blessed Trinity. We become, by grace, ever so gradually like God in how we love. The liturgy becomes, then, a foretaste of heaven. It is in this environment that "Christ Jesus is working in fullness for our transformation."

When we think about how the liturgy changes us, we must remember its two movements. Being attuned to the dynamics of sanctification and worship draws us into the very life of God,

---

16 Blessed Columba Marmion, *Christ in His Mysteries* (Bethesda, MD: Zaccheus Press, 2008), 173.
17 Ibid.

helping us as disciples into the divine current that will evangelize us throughout the whole of life.

To invest ourselves into the liturgical way of encountering God, we need two abilities. First, we must be able to receive what God offers us as the supernatural gifts that they are. Such an ability requires that we become consciously receptive, that we are able to recognize what God gives to be a gift, and to be drawn to gratitude for it. And, second, we must invest ourselves into the self-giving love offered to the Father that permeates every sacramental celebration. We must want to give a loving return to God.

It is important to note that investing ourselves into both receiving and giving requires effort and work on our part, distracted as we so frequently can be. Liturgical participation isn't intended to be an experience of passively receiving from God. Disciples ought not go to Mass only with the objective of "feeling fed," which we can equate with hearing a good homily, singing inspiring music, or experiencing the faith and friendliness of the community. We should certainly work hard for excellent homilies, music, and prayerfulness as a community. But the experience of encountering God ought not exclusively depend on these factors that are frequently the responsibility of other people. Rather, we must become active protagonists in receiving and giving, engaged in the work of sanctification and worship to our great good and to the glory of God.

I first became conscious of this twofold movement of love when I was fourteen years old, on the night when my life dramatically changed. After hearing the impassioned Palm Sunday invitation from my pastor to participate in the Sacred Triduum liturgies, I found myself sitting in the back of the church during the Holy Thursday liturgy. My pastor prayed the Eucharistic prayer intently, and the faith of the people around me was palpable. When the pastor lifted up the host and said, "Take this, all of you, and eat of it, for this is my body, which will be given up for you," I was able to see for the first time that this was real. I didn't then understand how, but Jesus himself was somehow present in our church that night, and what he was giving was nothing less than the gift of himself. As I joined the line to receive him in communion that night, the reality of this gift deeply impressed itself on me. And as our pastor began a Eucharistic procession, I joined that procession and remained deep into the night in Eucharistic adoration, because I knew I needed to give something significant back. I needed to give myself. Since coming to recognize these two movements of love, my life has not been the same.

4) Make the Church's incarnational language your own.

In everyday life, we communicate our thoughts and feelings — and give the gift of self — in ways that others can readily perceive: by speaking, listening, writing, serving, etc. In the sacraments, the upward and downward movements of love are expressed using this same language. God respects this language; he is, after all, its creator. He employs it (lifts it up) to make it possible for us human beings to give and receive divine love. The *Catechism* explains, "As a being at once body and spirit, [the human person] *expresses* and *perceives* spiritual realities through physical signs and symbols" (1146, emphasis added). What does this mean?

In our relationship with God, especially in the sacraments, we tangibly express our reverence by kneeling or standing or genuflecting. We indicate our remorse for our sins and need for mercy by approaching a specially consecrated human being, a priest, and confessing our specific sins. And we work at entrusting ourselves to God's providence by tithing and offering the gifts of bread and wine during the offertory. Each of these ritual actions conveys spiritual realities through the language of the body.

The reverse is also true: We perceive God's gift of himself to us in this language of signs and symbols. We hear his word, expressed in human words translated into our own language. We receive his forgiveness through some of the most beautiful words ever put to human language ("I absolve you of your sins … "). And what happens to that bread and wine brought to the altar during the offertory, representative as they are of our sacrifices and labors? They are divinized, and we then receive the gift of God himself under the appearances of bread and wine. Over a lifetime, we contemplate and marvel at this wondrous mystery, the transubstantiation of the bread and wine, which truly become the body, blood, soul, and divinity of Jesus Christ.

This sacramental language is a unique language. It is an ancient language. It is the language God has chosen to use in order to draw us to himself. Yet, if we don't know this language, we will likely fall into a hollow, mechanical ritualism, where these words and gestures are, for us, meaningless. However, when we learn this language, and choose to invest ourselves into it, we begin to give and receive the gift of love in ways that God has intended from the beginning of time.

5) Cooperate with sacramental grace so that the movement of divine love changes you.

"Go and sin no more!" These are the stirring words of Jesus to the woman caught in adultery after her transforming encounter with the mercy of God (cf. Jn 8:11). Her many sins have brought her before the Lord for judgment (or so her accusers think), but she is instead freed from her bondage to sin and its consequences. Yet, she is then directed to live from this wellspring of mercy in a new way. She is responsible now to live in alignment with the great gift she has been given. Her life must change; this is a command.

We hear similar words at the end of Mass. All four options

begin in the same way: "GO forth, the Mass is ended"; "GO and announce the Gospel of the Lord"; "GO in peace, glorifying the Lord by your life"; or just, "GO in peace."

This is not some ornamental way of saying "We're done here. You may depart." The "go" in the concluding rites of the Mass is the same "go" to the woman caught in adultery. And it is the same "go" of the great commission: "Go therefore and make disciples of all nations … " (Mt 28:18–20). The gravity of the saving action we encounter in the Mass requires us to live the Christian life in the world. Undeserved generosity by God must beget our own generosity of life. Conforming our lives to the gift we've received is expected by the One who first loved us. In his words to catechists in 2013, Pope Francis said: "The more that you unite yourself to Christ and he becomes the center of your life, the more he leads you out of yourself, leads you from making yourself the center and opens you to others."[18]

Sacramental living is meant to reshape us through a profound conversion of mind and heart. This renewal is not intended for me alone, but I am sent into my family and into the world to be a sanctifying influence for others, as I continue to grow as a disciple. It is a great problem, then, when we don't allow the grace received in sacramental encounters to challenge how we think and live, most particularly in our relationships with other people. Perhaps this disconnect sometimes originates in our mistaken belief that the sacraments are merely about me and God. We might think they are exclusively concerned with helping me be right with God and getting me to heaven. Yet, this is not the case; instead, the grace of the sacraments is meant to transform each of our relationships, leading us into the world to bear witness to the love and truth of the Gospel.

---

18 Pope Francis, Address of Holy Father Francis to Participants in the Pilgrimage of Catechists on the Occasion of the Year of Faith and of the International Congress on Catechesis (September 27, 2013), Vatican.va.

BEARING WITNESS TO RADICAL CHANGE

As we catechists invest more of ourselves into the sacramental life, with the Eucharist at its center, we are put into close contact with something extraordinary. Pope Emeritus Benedict XVI uses an unforgettable image to help us understand: "The substantial conversion of bread and wine into his body and blood introduces within creation the principle of a radical change, a sort of 'nuclear fission,' to use an image familiar to us today, which penetrates to the heart of all being, a change meant to set off a process which transforms reality, a process leading ultimately to the transfiguration of the entire world, to the point where God will be all in all (cf. 1 Cor 15:28)."[19] Living sacramentally puts us into remarkable closeness with the vivifying and transforming Presence of Christ in the Eucharist. This Eucharistic presence is the principle of radical supernatural change in the world, and it will also be so in our classrooms, conforming us more and more to how Jesus lives and teaches. Our authenticity in teaching others about the sacramental life must come from this deep reservoir of living Eucharistically. In this way, we can help others see how God is encountered in each of the sacraments. We can help them enter into the exchange of love that is the source of life. And they will be able to see how important it is to live the Christian life as beacons in a darkening world.

Saint John Vianney is revered for his heroic life as a parish priest. He deeply loved God through the sacraments and found strength in them to bring others to their transforming power. The final days of John Vianney are a compelling study. Sick, fragile, and unable to speak,

> in those last days his catechesis continued and
> was described as a series of exclamations ac-

---

[19] Pope Benedict XVI, *Sacramentum Caritatis*, accessed April 20, 2020, par. 11.

companied by tears. On the final day he ap-
peared in the parish church, his voice was no
longer audible to the crowds and so he simply
pointed repeatedly to the Tabernacle and wept.
All his catechesis, we might say had this goal
of leading every soul towards that wonder and
recognition expressed in words of the Second
Vatican Council that in the Blessed Eucharist is
found: "the whole spiritual good of the Church,
namely Christ himself, our Pasch" (*Presbytero-
rum Ordinis*, art. 5). It was with this last gesture
that the Curé of Ars fell silent in history, fell silent as a catechist.[20]

John Vianney's last catechesis is a stunning image of what is
needed in catechists today. We, too, must repeatedly point those
we teach to the transforming power of the sacramental encounter.

---

[20] Bishop Mark Davies, "St. John Vianney — A Saint of the New Evangelization, Part 3: The Holiness
of the Catechist," *The Catechetical Review* 4, no. 1 (January 2018): 27.

CHAPTER FOUR

Forming Missionary Disciples through Catechesis

A number of years ago, I found myself sitting in the back row of a catechist formation session, jotting down observations. One of my job responsibilities as diocesan coordinator of catechist formation was to help prepare and evaluate those who formed our diocesan catechists and religion teachers. As I watched one catechist's presentation, I was more and more impressed as the minutes ticked by. She taught with passion. Her love for God was tangible. Her knowledge of the Sacrament of Baptism, which she was teaching, was formidable. And her audience of catechists and religion teachers was alert and responsive.

Afterward, the presenter came and sat with me and asked, "So, what did you think?" There were many positives to point out, and I took time with each of these. Then, I said to her, "I just have one question. As you were teaching about baptism, I noticed that you never mentioned Jesus." Without blinking, she responded, "Oh, I wouldn't have done that. We did Jesus in the last course I taught for this group, about two months ago."

There was no doubt that this catechist, who had an extraordinary grasp of the content of the Faith, was accustomed to operating in a systematic way as a student of theology. First, we establish a Christ-centered, Trinitarian foundation, and then we build upon this foundation. Many of our textbooks and catechetical programs operate in this same way. However, if we are not frequently returning to the Person and Mystery of Jesus Christ as our central theme, as our most important content, our participants may not be making the connections to the foundation that we think they are. Many who have received years of catechetical instruction have left the Church behind, sometimes because they didn't understand what all the doctrine has to do with the love of Jesus.

We catechists must be singularly focused. Those we teach need to receive doctrinal richness and depth, but they also need to have placed before them, coherently and consistently, the invitation to communion with God and missionary discipleship. There need not be any false dichotomy here; it is unremittingly a "both/and" proposal. Our mission as catechists is to call people to discipleship and to form them as disciples. But if we are to be disciples, we have to make Christ's way of seeing our own way, which means doctrinal formation is important, too. After all, the Lord himself said, "If you love me, you will keep my commandments" (Jn 14:15).

Yet, what does it mean to be a disciple? Many helpful definitions and explanations abound today within Catholicism. I would like to propose this as a working definition: A missionary disciple is a person who lives in and from communion with God in Jesus.

As we have seen in the previous chapters, living in this communion (not passively, but actively) means that we consciously choose to abide in the Vine who is Christ, most essentially through a life of regular immersion in his word, intentional prayer, and sacramental practice, and in every way that Christ might be encountered. The disciple learns how to think, live, and love like Christ, who is our model of holiness. And we learn this from Christ himself, through being in close contact with him — by being joined to him — and by studying his word. Jesus, who is our one Mediator with the Father in the power of the Holy Spirit, brings us into loving communion with our Father in heaven, and this communion with God becomes the habitat of the disciple. Yet, especially for us as lay people, the world is also our habitat, because Jesus commanded his disciples to "go, therefore, and make disciples of all nations" (Mt 28:19).

Thus the disciple must also live from this reality of communion with God in Jesus (again, actively), because being in communion with God has implications for the rest of our life. Staying close to the light of Christ, the disciple is able to better see his own sins and imperfections, prompting ongoing conversion and change. But the disciple also learns to place his hope in Christ and in his grace alive within — grace that empowers a new way of turning outside of ourselves and loving others. The disciple's normative position of being in Christ gives him new vision, especially in how he sees other people. The disciple becomes a missionary in the everyday circumstances of life. God's own zeal for bringing others into the Love for which they were made becomes the primary catalyst of the disciple's heart.

This is not to say that disciples are flawless and already perfect in charity. Every disciple I've ever known (especially the one who looks back at me in the mirror) continues to struggle —

sometimes very profoundly — with ways of thinking and acting that obstruct our ability to love like Christ. Living in communion with God, however, gives us the potential to grow and to give of ourselves, even in radical ways — because the grace of God moves us to grow in the highest ways of love. As we read in 1 John 4:20, "If anyone says, 'I love God,' but hates his brother, he is a liar; for whoever does not love a brother whom he has seen cannot love God whom he has not seen." In these days of particularly strong vitriol between people who see the world differently, the missionary disciple is called to speak the truth, but always with great love and respect.

Renowned chastity speaker Jason Evert shares this story of a powerful exchange he had several years ago, which is a strong example of missionary love in action:

> A few years ago, I walked into a framing store with a large painting of Saint John Paul II, and laid it on the counter. The framer, a kind gentleman in his mid-forties, looked fondly on the image for a few moments, and remarked, "I'm a Catholic boy. Too bad the Church doesn't want me." Although it was unspoken, it was obvious he was referring to homosexuality. I asked, "What do you mean the Church doesn't want you? Of course the Church wants you. God loves you. The Church loves you. This is your home." He looked happily shocked asked, "What parish do *you* go to?"
>
> We had a pleasant conversation, and when I returned a few weeks later, I greeted him and he exclaimed, "You remembered my name!" We again entered into a warm conversation and I soon noticed tears in his eyes. He asked,

"Can I hug you?" "Absolutely!" I replied, and he walked around the counter and we embraced like brothers. I called over to my young son who was shopping with me, and said, "Give him a hug, too, buddy!" My boy wrapped his little arms around the man's legs and mine. Driving home, I thanked God for the meeting, because I *know* I had encountered Christ in this man. Those brief moments with him were the highlight of my day. He even sent me a message online to show how he framed the same painting of Saint John Paul II for his house!

EVANGELIZATION THROUGH CATECHESIS

We see the objective, but is it possible to form missionary disciples through catechesis?

The primary conviction underpinning these chapters is this: Teaching doctrinal content is insufficient on its own in catechesis. It is not enough to merely inform, even if done in inspiring ways. To be sure, the precious content of the Faith, which is entrusted to us for our teaching by the Lord himself, must be clear and unambiguous. It must be received and contemplated and gradually understood so that a responsiveness arises in the learner. But in today's challenging environment, merely explaining the Faith within catechesis is not enough.

Pope Francis drives this home in *The Joy of the Gospel*:

On the lips of the catechist the first proclamation must ring out over and over: "Jesus Christ loves you; he gave his life to save you; and now he is living at your side every day to enlighten, strengthen and free you." This first proclamation is called "first" not because it exists at the beginning and can then be forgotten or replaced by other more important things. It is first in a qualitative sense because it is the *principal* proclamation, the one which we must hear again and again in different ways, the one which we must announce one way or another *throughout* the process of catechesis, at every level and moment.[1]

Such a catechesis, then, envelops the teaching of the Faith with the proclamation of the love of Christ and the call to conversion. This proposal of discipleship must be ever-present as we teach, moving the mind and the heart. What is being described by Pope Francis is a catechesis that evangelizes.

The term "evangelization" itself is an ancient word, a translation of the Greek (*euangelion*) and Latin (*evangelium*), and the Old English (*godspel*), which means "glad tidings" or "Good News." Even if the word "evangelization" seems a bit tainted in our contemporary cultural context, it is the word Christ gave to his own teaching. It is, therefore, a word that is particularly precious to Christians. We encounter this word in Mark's account of the first moments of Jesus' public ministry. In Mark 1:15, the Lord uses three short sentences to sum up his mission: "This is the time of fulfillment. The kingdom of God is at hand. Repent, and believe in the Gospel" (*euangelion*). The evangelizing cate-

---

[1] Pope Francis, *Evangelii Gaudium*, accessed April 20, 2020, Vatican.va, par. 164, emphasis added. The Church's magisterial vision for catechesis has more and more emphasized the critical need for Catholic formation to be evangelistic. Whether it was Pope Saint Paul VI in 1975 taking the extraordinary step of describing catechesis as an irreplaceable element of the evangelization process, rather than a purely educative work (cf. *Evangelii Nuntiandi*, par. 17) or Pope Saint John Paul II, in his 1979 apostolic exhortation to catechists, insisting that the person of Jesus must be found at the center of catechesis (cf. *Catechesi Tradendae*, par. 5) or the 1997 *General Directory for Catechesis* calling catechesis a "means" of evangelization (par. 46) or Pope Emeritus Benedict XVI convoking the 2014 synod of bishops on the topic of the New Evangelization for the transmission of the Christian Faith and moving the oversight of catechetical ministry from the Congregation for the Clergy to the newly established Pontifical Council for Promoting New Evangelization, the magisterium has frequently insisted that evangelization and catechesis be carried out harmoniously.

chist, then, is one who, by teaching, accentuates Christ's words and deeds as the euangelion, the Good News, just as he did. At the same time, the evangelizing catechist realizes that, while Jesus' words and deeds are "Good News," truly receiving what he wishes to give also requires repentance. Giving the Good News of God's love, without also conveying the new way of life that this love necessitates, falls far short of what we read in the Gospels.

An insight from Bishop Robert Barron can be quite helpful here. Most of us presume that when the Lord urges repentance, he means turning away from immoral living. Bishop Barron points out that the original Greek term, *metanoiate,* was used here — and this word suggests that it is not merely moral change that is required (though the moral dimension is important), but rather a change that originates in the heart of each person, affecting every aspect of his existence. He explains, "The English word 'repent' has a moralizing overtone, suggesting a change in behavior or action, whereas Jesus' term seems to be hinting at a change at a far more fundamental level of one's being. ... What Jesus implies is this: the new state of affairs has arrived, the divine and human have met, but the way you customarily see is going to blind you to this novelty."[2]

Pope Saint John Paul II, in his resplendent encyclical on evangelization, *The Mission of the Redeemer,* points out just how necessary personal conversion is to the right reception of the Gospel: "The proclamation of the word of God has Christian conversion as its aim: a complete and sincere adherence to Christ and his Gospel through faith. ... Conversion means accepting, by a personal decision, the saving sovereignty of Christ and becoming his disciple."[3] We notice here that, for the evan-

---

[2] Robert Barron, *And Now I See: A Theology of Transformation* (New York: Crossroad, 1998), 4.
[3] John Paul II, *Redemptoris Missio,* accessed April 20, 2020, Vatican.va, par. 46.

gelized person, the only adequate response to the proclamation of God's word is *metanoia*. The evangelized person must choose to adhere, by faith, to Christ and his teaching. Christ must be placed in the position of highest authority, and such a decision requires that the whole of a person's life be reoriented.

God is always working for our conversion, even in ways difficult to immediately perceive. Many people do experience conversion in a "come to Jesus" moment upon hearing the Gospel proclaimed, or in the context of the sacraments, or by hearing the testimony of a believing person. We picture here the flash of light knocking Saul (soon to be Paul) off his horse. Quite frequently, though, the grace of God is moving us toward conversion less visibly, less overtly, less perceptibly. I think here of a character like the atheist Maurice Bendrix in Graham Greene's *The End of the Affair*. In this extraordinary novel, we see divine grace working ever so quietly and gradually in Sarah, moving her steadily out of an adulterous affair with Maurice and back to what is true and real. Maurice's ensuing darkness as a result of his abandonment seems to deepen as he turns more and more in on himself. And yet, the change in Sarah before her eventual death begins to fracture his unbelief, provoking new questions within him. The closing words of the novel, while dark, reveal something new very slowly beginning to emerge in Maurice, to that point in the story a militant atheist: "O God, You've done enough, You've robbed me of enough, I'm too tired and old to learn to love, leave me alone for ever."[4] Maurice's prayer is raw and real. But God is not afraid of our anger, which is quite frequently for us a first step toward healing. For Maurice, such a prayer reveals the beginnings of belief.

Another example of gradual conversion occurs in the story of retired autoworker Walt Kowalski (played by Clint Eastwood)

[4] Graham Greene, *The End of the Affair* (New York: Penguin Books, 1995), 192.

in the 2008 film *Gran Torino*. Cantankerous and ill-natured, Walt is continually pursued by his parish priest, who made a promise to Walt's wife on her deathbed that he would get Walt to confession. Strained in his relationships with his children and grandchildren, Walt's edginess escalates when a large Hmong family from Cambodia moves into the house next door. In a dramatic turn, Walt unexpectedly protects one of these neighbors, young Thao, from being recruited by a violent gang. Consequently, Walt is drawn into a surprising friendship with his neighbors, who revere him for protecting Thao. Through his horror at a terrible crime perpetrated by the gang near the end of the movie, divine grace does move Walt into the confessional and into the ultimate act of self-sacrificial love.

These are but two illustrations of the great mysterious movement of grace indicated by the term *metanoia*. The Christian — indeed every person — must move out of a purely self-referential way of seeing, thinking, and acting and into the generous self-sacrificial way of living demonstrated by our Exemplar, Christ Jesus. We can be assured that God is working toward this great good in every person, through every life circumstance. But our free cooperation is necessary in order for conversion to be realized, even if this cooperation happens gradually, slowly, and in stages, as it so often does.

When it comes to our own proclamation and teaching of the truth of Christ, metanoia is what Our Lord asks of both us and our students. Reflecting on the words of John Paul II in *The Mission of the Redeemer*, Ralph Martin notes the demand that metanoia places on our efforts for the New Evangelization:

> At parish and diocesan levels, people commonly talk about the new evangelization as "getting people to come to Mass again," or "getting them active in the parish." While these are good

things, unfortunately we also have people coming to Mass or active in the parish who are not
converted, according to the definition of John
Paul II above. His definition of conversion includes a "complete and sincere adherence to
Christ and his Gospel," and "accepting by a personal decision, the saving sovereignty of Christ
and becoming his disciple." To surrender to the
Lordship of Christ by a conscious, personal decision is no little thing! To consciously decide to
be a disciple, to place one's trust in Jesus, to embrace his teachings, and to follow him wherever
he may lead, is indeed a worthy and challenging
definition of conversion.[5]

The evangelizing catechist, then, teaches the Faith by proposing
it as Good News and bears witness to the necessity of conversion
of life. The call to change, to deeper faith, to an embrace of the
Church's teaching, to repentance, to intentional charity, to living
life in the newness of the kingdom of God — these are the un-
dercurrents operating within the Christian disciple. This move
away from self and into the love of God isn't achieved in an in-
stant but is a lifelong quest. It will not only change how we pray
and participate in the liturgy, but will make us less self-centered
and more able to put others before ourselves. In serving the
good of others, the disciple conforms herself to the way of Our
Lord, "who, though he was in the form of God, did not regard
equality with God something to be grasped. Rather, he emptied
himself, taking the form of a slave" (Phil 2:6–7). This life of self-
emptying love is the essence of what it means to follow Jesus.

For young children, the invitation to discipleship must be

---

5 Ralph Martin, "What Is the New Evangelization?" *The Catechetical Review* 1, no. 1 (January 2015): 6.

introduced in its essentials, without artificialities and complications. The catechist must be sure not to underestimate a child's capacities for contact with God. In fact, it is in childhood that "spiritual instincts"[6] must be developed, which become a foundation for relationship with God for the rest of life. As children grow in maturity, their minds must be engaged more deeply. As teenagers and young adults, they will need to study the teaching of Christ and the Church to learn how to think and live in consistency with the One with whom they are united, amidst the complexities and contradictions of our fallen, postmodern world. A robust engagement with the teaching of Christ — in all of its demand and splendor — is more important for young people and adults than ever before.

This brings us to an important question: Many today wonder whether we should evangelize before attempting to catechize. Should a person be responsive to the basic Gospel message and the call to conversion before being taught more extensively? Certainly there is merit to promoting evangelization opportunities before and after periods of formal catechesis, as well as in the first weeks of every cycle of catechesis. But it is important here to become convicted, with the Church, that catechesis itself can be an evangelizing initiative. In fact, this is the hope and wise counsel of the Church to us catechists today — to reconfigure our teaching in ways that stir up a desire for God and a decision for discipleship as we unambiguously teach the essentials of the content of the Faith.

CONVERSION AND FREEDOM

Saint John Paul II famously wrote, "The definitive aim of catechesis is to put people not only in touch but in communion,

---

[6] See Blessed Marie-Eugene of the Child Jesus, "The Child's Potential for Contact with God," trans. by Teresa Hawes, *The Sower* 35:3, July 2014, 32–33.

in intimacy, with Jesus Christ."[7] Strictly speaking, the catechist cannot put anyone into communion with Christ. The intimate friendship with God described by John Paul II can only be brought about as a person freely chooses to accept the gift of such communion. This means our learners must, in their development, frequently will this relationship for themselves, if it is going to be established and remain through their adult life.

Unlike previous generations of Catholics, today's young people rarely choose or sustain communion with God simply because "the Church says it" or "my parents want this for me." Rather, young people today will open themselves to union with God and seek to make this union the hinge-point of their life once they have encountered Christ and perceived his invitation to intimate communion and to mission. Their desire to live as disciples will arise from this encounter. And once this desire arises, it must be acted upon, willed, chosen for oneself.

Consequently, a catechesis that merely explains, even if it also proclaims, will not form missionary disciples. When catechesis fixates on the purely explanatory, the content of Christianity remains theoretical, at a distance from the learner and not properly his or her own. Opportunities also must abound — from a very early age — for young people to take steps forward on their own in freedom. For instance, children's book author Maura Roan McKeegan has an important insight to share with parents seeking to form their children by reading books with them in the home. Inviting children to read engages the freedom of a child in a way that operating by mandate does not — and the effects can be very positive. McKeegan writes:

> Look for a time when the child isn't distracted
> by other things and warmly invite him to read

---

[7] John Paul II, *Catechesi Tradendae*, accessed April 20, 2020, Vatican.va, par. 5.

> with you. It's important to make reading a joy
> and not a chore, because a child might resent
> reading if he's forced to do it when he wants to
> be somewhere else. If reading is a treat — if he
> gets to stay up ten minutes past bedtime in or-
> der to read a book with you, or if he gets spe-
> cial time with you after lunch to snuggle up in a
> comfortable spot and read together — then the
> child will forever connect reading books with
> feelings of safety, comfort, and love.[8]

In the same way, in our catechesis of little ones, as they grow
into greater spiritual maturity, there are always choices we can
offer them. Perhaps they can be given options for an opening
or closing prayer, or an activity that will be done to apply the
material. I had the great joy several years ago to visit the Notre
Dame de Vie institute in southern France and to visit a school
where the institute's catechetical program, Come Follow Me, was
being employed. As I observed the teacher with the children, I
was particularly struck by the choice offered at the end of the
catechesis. The catechist led the group in a time of silent prayer;
and then, after some moments in silence, she quietly told them
that they were welcome to stay in silence with God for as long as
they liked. But they could also move into the next room and participate in an activity related to the theme of the catechesis. I was
astounded at — what seemed to me at that time — the novelty of
offering children a choice between two goods as they are being
taught. Many of these little ones chose to stay in silent prayer.
Others participated in a theme-related activity and discussion. It
wasn't difficult to see that being regularly presented this choice

---

[8] Maura Roan McKeegan, "Reading with Love: Tips for Sharing Spiritual Books with Children,"
St. Paul Center, August 14, 2009, https://stpaulcenter.com/reading-with-love-tips-for-sharing
-spiritual-books-with-children/

was to their good. They were personally invested because their freedom was engaged.[9]

These opportunities to freely respond (as we proclaim and teach) are essential for participants to make the Faith their own. There is no decision for discipleship without freedom. One 1950s writer argues for what he calls a "pedagogy of liberty." Jean Mouroux explains, "If we can nurture in a man or a child the emergence and the victory of spiritual liberty, we have accomplished our task. If not, all is lost and the Christian life will weaken into childishness; it will harden into formalism; and finally it will disappear."[10]

APPRENTICESHIP: THE WAY TO DISCIPLESHIP

Those being formed through catechesis need to be apprenticed into the Christian life.[11] They need to be shown the way to discipleship by real people who care for them. We catechists need to do all we can to empower parents to be the primary mentors in the Christian life for their children; but catechists, too, can play an important role.

Many today put great hope in youth ministries to create opportunities for missionary discipleship formation, and rightfully so. But every avenue of catechesis must be a place of transformative teaching, whether it is in the home, in the par-

---

[9] For additional examples of how Come Follow Me creates an atmosphere of discovery and freedom for the child in catechesis, see Sister Hyacinthe Defos du Rau, OP, "Come Follow Me: A New Model for Children's Catechesis" in James C. Pauley, *Liturgical Catechesis in the 21st Century: A School of Discipleship* (Chicago: Liturgy Training Publications, 2017), 145–64.

[10] Jean Mouroux, *From Baptism to the Act of Faith*, trans. Sister M. Elizabeth, IHM, and Sister M. Johnice, IHM (Boston: Allyn and Bacon, 1964), 22.

[11] The Second Vatican Council adopts this idea of "apprenticeship" in describing the catechetical formation required in the catechumenal process by which adults are prepared for the sacraments of initiation. "Ad Gentes," art. 14, states: "The catechumenate is not a mere expounding of doctrines and precepts," important though this is, "but a training period in the whole Christian life, and an apprenticeship duty drawn out, during which disciples are joined to Christ their Teacher."

ish, or in the Catholic school. A teaching colleague of mine, Dr. Amy Roberts, who is a Catholic high school teaching veteran, is deeply convicted that the Catholic school can be a place of profound evangelization. In addition to focusing the identity of a Catholic school and the content of its academics around the call to discipleship, many opportunities arise each day for discipling students. Amy gives us this example:

> I recall one high school senior, whom I will call "Bob." While Bob was Catholic, neither he nor his family attended Mass or participated in parish activities. I had taught Bob as a sophomore, and remembered him as rowdier and more immature than most of his peers. As a senior, his sophomoric behaviors had evolved into a pattern of aggressive interrogation of me, sometimes on topic, many times off. I always tried to answer sincere questions, but not to allow them to derail the class or foster disrespect. Bob's questions frequently fell into the latter categories: the ludicrous, the dangerous, the disrespectful. One day he began arguing that legalized marijuana and recreational marijuana usage were morally good options, resulting in his classmates' visible frustration and exasperation with his efforts to interfere with the class. When the bell rang, I asked him to stay behind. I sat down in the desk next to him and said, "What was that about?" He began, "I'm just trying to get people to think; nobody wants to think." I said, "I have friends who once believed what you said today. And they now suffer the ill effects of marijuana us-

age, and regret their decision bitterly. I don't want to see you go through the same thing." And suddenly, his aggressive manner dissolved. His facial expression changed, as did his tone of voice. Out came a story of sinful choices, betrayal, regret. I listened carefully. Our time was limited, so I could only express my sorrow over his pain, my promise of prayers, and my admonition that he could not continue to disrupt class in this way. But I paid closer attention to what he said in class after that. While he still asked hard questions, they were on topic and without the aggressive, "I dare you to prove it" manner that he had shown previously. A couple of weeks later I kept him after class again, this time to follow up. "Your comments and questions are showing me that you are wounded by these experiences," I said. A nervous, wobbly grin on his face, he looked me in the eye and said, "No one has ever said that to me before. This tells me you actually care about me. What do I do?" I directed him to confession as well as to counseling. He graduated and moved away soon after that, and I have not heard from him in the years since. But I do know that for one brief period, a teacher had an open door to speak into his life and heart, to use the occasion for discipline as an opportunity to disciple.

Amy's story brings us to an important facet of making disciples: the formative influence catechists have in the lives of the people they teach. The catechist-disciple is someone who is bringing faith and life together within themselves; and therefore, is able to be a credible teacher and guide in the way of conversion and discipleship.

In a 2015 book, Jim Beckman identifies four essential steps for just such an apprenticeship process.[12] Taking inspiration from his model, let's develop what these steps could look like for the catechist and learner:

1. **Teach.** First, of course, we teach. The catechist is a teacher. The content of the Faith originates not in ourselves; it emerges not from our own experience; but it is, in fact, revealed. There is a content to Christianity that our students need to hear and engage with, and to which they need to respond.

2. **Show.** To live the Catholic life, our students have to actually see intimacy with God embodied in real human beings. There are two ways to show this life to them. The first is through the testimony of those who are living it, who have experience and wisdom to share. The theological concept of co-operating with grace, for instance, becomes something I want to do when I see its fruits realized in another person who can authentically describe for me the process. We "show," therefore, when we can offer a personal account of what we teach. If we can't speak from our own experience, perhaps there is another person in the room or in the parish (or from a family of one of our learners) who might be able to offer a compelling testimony. Of

---

[12] Jim Beckman, "Rethinking Youth Ministry," in Sherry Weddell, ed., *Becoming a Parish of Intentional Disciples* (Huntington, IN: Our Sunday Visitor, 2015), 117–37.

course, showing the Faith lived is exactly the point of turning to the testimonies of the saints.

The second way to show is to actually help learners see and experience whatever is being taught. As we teach them about the Eucharist, for example, we can bring them to the reverent silence of Eucharistic adoration. If we're teaching them about Christ's love for the poor, we can spend time serving with them in a soup kitchen or a nursing home. Helping them to see Catholicism lived is vital to learning to live it ourselves.

3. **Try.** In order for a real change of life to be possible, our students must have opportunities to put into practice what we've taught and shown them. How can we help them try to pray as we've prepared them? Perhaps there's a chance for them to attempt an answer to a challenging objection to the Faith. If they've encountered the Lord in a compelling way, can we help them put this powerful experience into their own words so they can share it with others? If we do not challenge young people to take steps forward in real-to-life ways, our catechesis isn't going to help them form new instincts and habits. And it is precisely these instincts and habits that help a person to flourish as a disciple.

4. **Do.** What we repeatedly try, with accountability to see us through the experiences of failure, gradually becomes a confident ability that we ourselves possess. Living intentionally as a disciple develops from frequent experiences of growing in the habits of discipleship. The final measure of our collective

efforts as families, parishes, and schools to form
others in the Faith is found in our answer to this
challenging question: Are we empowering those
we teach to live the Christian life independently?
Have we given them the focused preparation they
need in order to grow in union with God and as
followers of Jesus after they have left the encouraging environs of our faith communities?

In this apprenticeship model, therefore, we teach and show so
that they can try and do. The catechist, then, helps others begin to walk so they can very soon run on their own. It looks a
bit like what Jake Stanley of Gilbert, Arizona, describes in his
recent experience as a youth minister:

A few months ago, a teen whom I had never
met walked into my office. He said that he had
no real faith background, but that he had done
a little reading and decided he wanted to know
more about becoming Catholic. I spent some
time getting to know him and, following that
day, we started getting together once a week to
talk and discuss the Faith.

Rather than just overwhelm him with information about all of the Church's teachings
in these meetings, I spent a lot of time asking
him questions such as, "Who do you think Jesus is?" and "Why do you think Jesus founded a Church?" As he shared his thoughts, he
became more interested in the topics and engaged in meaningful dialogue about them.

We began reading the Gospel of Matthew
together, one chapter per week, and we both

shared our reflections and questions in response to the readings. These conversations
became very fruitful and helped this student
take the next step in his relationship with the
Lord.

During this process, this teen began coming to weekly Mass with my family. I taught
him how to make the sign of the cross and
genuflect, what Holy Water is for, and about
the Liturgy of the Word and the Liturgy of
the Eucharist. He told me he was shocked at
how much the Church felt like a family from
his first Mass on. He was blown away and
loved coming so much that he rode his bike or
walked all the way to the church every Sunday!

What do we see in Jake's story? He invested time. The catechesis
was conversational. By studying God's word together with the
young man, Jake modeled Scripture study for him and gave
him opportunities to become comfortable reading and praying
with Scripture himself. Jake also helped him understand sacramental language and how to pray sacramentally. Finally, Jake
certainly did some teaching and showing, but he also created
opportunities within the supportive community of his parish
and his own family for this young man to grow in understanding and confidence.

Apprenticeship is necessary if disciples are to be formed.
This means that a mentoring approach must be incorporated
into our catechetical models and methods. The next five chapters will engage the question of how to plan a catechesis that
evangelizes and builds up disciples. As we consider such a catechesis, we need to keep before us the importance of "teaching,"
"showing," "trying," and "doing." Whatever methods we employ

as catechists, the "marks" of apprenticeship need to be prominent. They will be in the coming pages.

Part II
A Catechesis That Evangelizes

In his helpful 1997 book, *The Mystery We Proclaim*, Monsignor Francis Kelly suggests, in broad terms, a five-step method of catechesis that many have used over the years to good effect.[1] We will reflect on this method of teaching, because it provides concrete opportunities for much of what has been suggested more theoretically in the previous chapter. This model promotes a culture of conversion and discipleship, first and foremost, by taking steps to allow the word of God to have its full authority and power in each catechesis.

The five steps of the ecclesial method are:

- Preparation
- Proclamation
- Explanation
- Application
- Celebration

The first step (preparation) helps participants into a position of openness and receptivity to what will be proclaimed. Next, the ecclesial method does not begin with a didactic exposition, but rather a proclamation of the essential foundational truth for the lesson as the Good News that it is. What is proclaimed is then unpacked and thoughtfully explored (explanation) before it is applied to culture and proposed in the context of personal discipleship (application). Finally, the content of the Faith is reflected upon in its goodness and beauty, with the possibility that joy and gratitude are aroused and deepened (celebration). Directed as it is toward personal transformation, the ecclesial method of catechesis provides not only for deeper understanding of the doctrinal content being taught, but also for the responsiveness

---

[1] See Monsignor Francis D. Kelly, *The Mystery We Proclaim — Second Edition: Catechesis for the Third Millennium* (Huntington, IN: Our Sunday Visitor, 1997). The first edition of this book, published before the writing of the 1997 *General Directory for Catechesis,* was published in 1993.

to God that is the terrain of missionary discipleship.

In the next five chapters, we will consider each of these steps, re-envisioning them more broadly and flexibly as essential movements that will be present in any evangelizing catechesis, no matter the lesson-planning approaches being employed. Each of the five movements described is important, but so is our personal creativity, flexibility, and a loving awareness of our students and their needs. It may well be that these are not followed as sequential steps. It may also be that the five movements are spread out over the course of a week or a unit in a Catholic school context. What is important in this is ensuring our catechesis gives as real an opportunity as possible for an encounter with the word, as well as encouragement and help in responding to that encounter.

Exploring these five movements of a discipleship-based catechesis will provide helpful insights, not only to those who work in Catholic schools and in parish children's catechesis, but also to those who plan youth ministry, Bible studies, or RCIA. Parents and grandparents will also find here a helpful arc for their own primary, informal, everyday catechesis within the home.

Catechesis helps something new take root, grow, and eventually flourish. Inspired by Our Lord's recourse to the image of soil, seed, and fruitfulness, these five movements will be presented with this important analogy in mind. Let's now seek to make our own a practical skillset, which can be put to immediate use in crafting a catechesis that evangelizes and invites to discipleship.

CHAPTER FIVE

Preparation
Attending to the Soil

A ny good gardener knows that the growth process does not begin with the planting of the seed. Rather, the gardener must first attend to the soil into which the seed will be planted. Soil conditions vary greatly, and may require work. Hard ground first needs to be tilled. The rocks and weeds have to be removed. The dirt may need to be supplemented and fortified. These initial efforts are important because once the seed is planted, it will need a nourishing environment to have a chance to thrive. Of course, this exact process from the natural world is mirrored in the supernatural work of "sowing" the word of God. Jesus himself described the importance of receiving the Word and the various ways the human heart can be opened or obstructed to the seed of the Word (cf. Mk 4:3–9).

So, what do adverse "soil conditions" look like today, practically speaking? If you became Catholic as an adult, did you ever find yourself attending an evening RCIA session exhausted and thinking about other things? Or perhaps if you went to Catholic school, your disinterest in your religion class could partly be attributed to its placement between language arts and social studies, making it seem that the study of God in his Trinitarian life and in human history is just another class. As a catechist, maybe you've seen the look on the face of a young woman who is forced by her parents to attend a retreat. Or perhaps you've been greeted by blank stares from people who seem truly indifferent. We are all familiar with the hard, rocky ground of parish and school catechesis.

The catechist's first conviction should be that each person who walks through the door is preoccupied and uninterested. Many might prefer to be elsewhere. As they enter this place where the Word of God is to be encountered, we have to first help them in their need to transition to a new interior place.

Timothy O'Malley, drawing upon the educational wisdom of Monsignor Luigi Giussani, suggests that what is needed first is "provocation." Of course, he doesn't mean that the catechist "provokes" in a negative way by hurling insults or picking fights. Rather, especially in the first stages of catechesis, each person needs to be drawn to the important questions, to ask them for himself. Each needs to be awakened from within. The "educational task of provocation brings us face-to-face with the 'really real,' with the questions that matter. Provocation is the first step of seeing the world even in all its messiness for what it is — a gift to be contemplated."[1]

---

[1] Timothy P. O'Malley, *Divine Blessing: Liturgical Formation in the RCIA* (Collegeville, MN: Liturgical Press, 2019). O'Malley offers the example of holding one's newborn child. "Anyone who has held a newborn child can recognize the way that this experience provokes us towards the deeper questions: what really matters now that this child exists in my life? How will I live after this encounter?" (7). The author here references the work of Monsignor Luigi Giussani, *The Religious Sense*, trans. John Zucchi (Montreal: McGill-Queen's University Press, 1997), 101.

Monsignor Kelly describes something quite similar, explaining that "the first step of authentic catechesis must be to help people overcome and step out of this self-absorbed environment and into the bright sunlight of the living and loving God."[2] Moving into this new position is not automatic for most of us and cannot be achieved without some effort and foresight. As catechists, we can't presume that a quick "hello" and even quicker opening prayer will accomplish this. Is there anything we can do to help them lean forward in their seats, interested and alert to the precious Faith that we will share with them?

THE EFFORTS OF THE CATECHIST

There are three important questions we need to consider in this initial movement of preparation. First, how can we help participants to temporarily disengage from distractions and be as fully present to the catechetical experience as possible? Second, how can we stir up curiosity regarding our subject matter before we start teaching it? And third, how can we help participants to become attuned to the presence and inspiration of Christ the Teacher?

An insight from Kelly helps us keep a correct perspective with the potential and the limits of what we are working to achieve. He writes, "The catechist must help create the conditions for the possibility of a deepening of God's Word."[3] Notice that the catechist does not deepen God's Word in people. All that the catechist can do is to create the conditions for the possibility of God's Word being deepened in people's hearts. The task of deepening is a work of the Holy Spirit — and it must be freely undertaken by each individual person.

What, then, are the conditions over which the catechist has some influence?

---

[2] Kelly, *The Mystery We Proclaim*, 140.
[3] Ibid., 138.

First Condition: A "Provocative" Environment

It is a deeply Catholic intuition to treat the place where God is encountered in a sacramental way. Take, for example, Bishop Robert Barron's description of the experience of setting foot in a Gothic cathedral:

> When one enters a Gothic cathedral, one is plunged into darkness. As the eyes struggle to adjust from the relative brightness outside to the dimness of the interior, one is practically blinded. During my time in France, I often witnessed the phenomenon of people stumbling and groping helplessly as they passed through the portals of a cathedral. The difficulty comes, not only from the natural incapacity of the eyes, but from the fact that the darkest portion of the interior is precisely near the main doors. None of this, of course, is by accident. The Gothic architects wanted to impress something of terrible spiritual moment upon the minds of those who visited the cathedrals: we are a people who walk in darkness. ... We may enter the door with confidence, sure of our direction and purpose, but the moment we step into the cathedral, we are disoriented, lost, desperately in need of a guide.
>
> What is wonderful is that the cathedral itself emerges as that guide. Just as Christ blinded Saul and then sent him help in the person of Ananias, so the cathedral casts us into the shadows and then shows us the light. As we move through the church — with hesitation at first — we come to ever greater illumination,

the windows allowing more and more light into
the space. The spiritual lesson is clear: as long
as we sinners stay in the confines of the church,
we will make our way to the Light; when we try
to walk outside the church, our blindness only
intensifies.[4]

We create beautiful churches because the building itself can reveal something of the invisible world that is sacramentally made present. Being in such a "provocative" space can help us gain proper supernatural perspective and enter readily into the liturgical encounter.

The catechetical setting, where we seek deeper understanding of the gift of Christ's life and teaching, is a sacred place as well. Christ is present here, and the People of God join together for a most important purpose. Therefore, the setting ideally ought to reflect something of this presence and this purpose in catechesis. Of course, catechesis will not take place in a location that even faintly resembles a Gothic cathedral, but more likely will be situated in a cluttered school classroom or a musty parish hall. Therefore, some creativity and planning are required when it comes to the atmosphere of the place. Challenging teaching spaces such as these need not sink our ship.

What can we do so that an environment that would ordinarily work against transformative catechesis instead is made to work in our favor? Ideally, when a person enters, it should feel like a sacred place where God may be encountered and where the Word of God is revered and studied. When a place affects us in this way, it can open within us new expectancies. While there are many ways to create such an atmosphere, these three

---

[4] Robert Barron, *Heaven in Stone and Glass: Experiencing the Spirituality of the Great Cathedrals* (New York: Crossroad Publishing Co., 2002), 21–23.

practices are particularly helpful:

- Bring beauty into the classroom. Beauty attracts. It provokes. It draws us out of ourselves. It brings a certain light and peace to the spirit, since it expresses something of the radiance of God. Every investment we make into creating a setting where beauty reaches to us is worth the time and energy. Perhaps we can display and teach from a work of sacred art, a piece that, when carefully studied, brings wonder or delight. Some parishes have worked to build lending libraries of works of art for catechists to use as they are teaching various topics or when seeking to accentuate various liturgical seasons or feast days. What if, as they entered the room, music was playing softly, setting the space apart through our sense of hearing? Are there ways to introduce natural beauty into the catechetical environment, perhaps by adding plants or flowers or pictures of beautiful places?

- Create a focal point for prayer and a visual reminder of the presence of God. We also need reminders that we are drawing close to God when we enter into prayer and study his Word. On a table, we could include a Trinitarian image or a statue of Jesus or a standing crucifix or a painting that lends to the dignity of the space. We human beings need sacramental, visual, tangible reminders that put us in touch with the Father, the Son, and the Holy Spirit. A nicely designed table arrangement with a standing crucifix, a tablecloth or sheet (perhaps with a color corresponding to the liturgical season), a lit candle, and an open Bible can help us pray well and deepen our awareness of the presence of God among us and in his Word.

• Arrange desks or seats in a way that promotes personal connection. We've all been in rooms where it is easy for learners to remain distant and isolated. Every experienced teacher knows the importance of being in close proximity to those being taught. In catechesis, this is important not only to keep people engaged and reduce discipline issues, but also to foster apprenticeship. The catechist is a living witness, and the Faith being handed on is the "pearl of great price" (cf. Mt 13:46). We are seeking to apprentice our students in the Christian life, and such an apprenticeship happens best when we are close to students, making frequent eye contact and able to engage them more personally.

Atmosphere and expectation go hand in hand. For parents who are seeking to be the first catechists for their children, a warm and engaging environment within the home is at least as impor- tant as it is for the parish or school catechist. Parents can arrange sacred places within the home where personal connection and anticipation for the things of God become more likely. Alison Oertle of Scottsdale, Arizona, describes just such a tradition she has with her family when they gather to grow in faith together:

"Preparation" here almost always means gathering around a table. I know I will have eager participation and bodies ready to linger if I take a few minutes to make a pot of tea, set out a tray of something sweet, and simply light a candle. It doesn't have to be complicated or made from scratch; store-bought cookies are eaten just as readily. Without my having to call them, the seats are filled and there is a sense of anticipation that good things are coming. They don't want to miss out on this special time. This perfectly sets the stage to encounter the sweetness of the Lord through Scripture sharing, reading the life of a saint, or deepening our understanding and application of Church teaching.

Second Condition: Our Disposition toward Our Students

Our presence as the catechist in the classroom is another condition over which we have a great deal of influence. When our students see our smile, feel our respect, sense our joy and good humor, and know our authenticity, they are better disposed to hear us and open themselves to what we're trying to teach them. Ginny Casey, a high school teacher in College Station, Texas, provides us an example of just how impactful a teacher's presence can be to fruitful catechesis:

> As a religion teacher, I tried to establish an atmosphere of solidarity in my classroom. If the girls couldn't have two ear piercings, then neither would I. If they couldn't use their cell phones, then I would demonstrate by putting mine away. If they couldn't eat in the classroom, then I would

do my best not to eat in front of them.

One day I was feeling faint, so I stealthily tried to pull a Fruit Roll-Up out of my lunch box. One of my students saw me and became overwhelmed by a craving for a Fruit Roll-Up. With much drama in her voice, she commented on how desperately she wanted one after seeing mine, so I just gave it to her. Not for answering a question correctly, not while at the same time warning her that the wrapper had better make it to the trash; I just gave it to her as if she were my peer and we shared the same lunch table. She asked many times if I was "serious" when I handed it to her and then told me that I had made her day. She said she might cry and I thought she was again being dramatic; but after she thanked me later, I discovered that she had a very hard day. She said, "Mrs. Casey, you always talk about the dignity of the human person and solidarity and that is how you treat us — you treat us like real people."

We ourselves hopefully have people in our lives who humble us by their generosity, who just by their presence can immediately bring down our walls and move us back to what is most important. Fostering a good, healthy relationship with our students can provide this for them, too.

From a supernatural perspective, often our disposition toward God while we teach is our most important quality. Modeling for participants that the Lord is present and may be encountered through prayer, through moments of silence, and in the words and insights of other people is a strong encouragement for them to likewise seek him.

Third Condition: Their Disposition toward One Another

Finally, when the group of learners becomes a genuine community of friends, new horizons open up for the group. As they are able to truly be themselves and build connection and friendships with each other, an environment of encounter and conversion is established.

I won't forget the night many years ago when I was teaching confirmation students, and I noticed immediately that "Alec" was unusually nervous and self-absorbed. A little later I found out that some other kid had challenged him to a fight as they were walking into the parish hall. Under such circumstances, is there any possibility that either young man was open or able to truly hear that night? What about the rest of the group, as word gradually spread through the room?

Every effort to strengthen community, so that the baptismal reality of being made brother and sister to one another becomes tangible, has profound catechetical benefits. Imagine the kinds of conversations inside and outside of catechesis that may be had when an atmosphere of trust and respect prevails. What we want is for a genuine community of friends to develop.

Becca Arend recently experienced the convergence of all three of these conditions (making a provocative space for learning, being an inviting presence, and fostering community among participants) at an adult evangelization series run in her Halifax, Nova Scotia, parish:

> One of my parishioners has a flair for decor, and every week she prepared thoughtful and unique table centerpieces and room lighting. A handful of incredible ladies prepared a home-cooked meal each week for all fifty-five participants. When our non-Christian guests walked

into the parish hall, they felt less like they were in a church basement and more like they were invited to a dinner. They were bombarded with hospitality and love from the team, ate a delicious meal, and had a pleasant dinner conversation, so by the time the video and discussion began, many of them had let their guard down. One of those former atheists is now a leader in the program, on fire with the love of Christ, trying to convince her husband and coworkers to come join us in that church basement.

Creating a setting reflective of Christ's sacred presence, enlivened by personal connections with both the catechist and with other learners, does not guarantee an evangelizing catechesis. But these are important first steps in cultivating the soil.

FIRST WORDS: STIRRING UP CURIOSITY

Apart from creating an atmosphere conducive to fruitful catechesis, how do we begin our catechesis?

This may come as a surprise, considering the short time we have with them, but in the first five to ten minutes, we shouldn't teach them anything. This first movement, after all, is all about the soil. First, therefore, we should do something to personally connect with the group and help them be present. A friendly welcome, a smile, an inquiry about what's going on in life, a game or icebreaker, a quick story ... each of these is a potential way to establish connection. Active and thoughtful participation in catechesis frequently depends upon whether this connection is first established. If we can get them to laugh, to answer a question, to tell a story (each of these is a way of getting participants to be verbal), engaging them throughout the catechesis becomes much more likely. Many catechists become frustrated by groups who sit back passively and don't speak. Very often this happens because we haven't set the tone in the opening minutes that their voices will be important.

Next, we must provoke their curiosity about what we will teach. What would it take to make them want to understand more about the theme of the catechesis before we even begin teaching it? It is fascinating to read through the Gospels with an eye to just how often Our Lord triggered curiosity as a teacher. When I read the parable of the sower, I am frequently struck by a twist at the end of the story that seems, at face value, to be rather absurd from our perspective as teachers. In Mark 4:3–9, we read:

> "Hear this! A sower went out to sow. And as he sowed, some seed fell on the path, and the birds came and ate it up. Other seed fell on rocky ground where it had little soil. It sprang up at once because the soil was not deep. And when the sun rose, it was scorched and it withered for lack of roots. Some seed fell among thorns, and the thorns grew up and choked it and it produced no grain. And some seed fell on rich soil and produced fruit. It came up and grew and yielded thirty, sixty, and a hundredfold." He added, "Whoever has ears to hear ought to hear."

When does the Lord explain the meaning of the parable to the people? He doesn't! In fact, he dismisses the crowd with no explanation. He explains its meaning to his disciples, but not to his broader audience.

Why would he do such a thing? Doesn't any good teacher want to promote understanding, to help make connections? How could he just leave them there? While Jesus did frequently explain, in this case he did not. Perhaps he did so to "provoke" them. I like to hope that, had I been in the crowd, hearing this parable would have propelled me into numerous conversations with family and friends. Ultimately, I hope, it would have motivated me to step forward to seek answers from Jesus himself.

How, then, can we rouse curiosity? James Bitting, a high school teacher in Wichita, Kansas, tells of one way he does so:

> I have a realistic-looking skull on my desk. I position it to be facing the students (it's constantly "looking" at them). I acquired the skull a few years ago from a science classroom closet. It had been used for teaching anatomy class but hadn't been used for many years and was collecting dust. I took it (with permission) and placed it on my desk. Students immediately started noticing the skull and asking, "Mr. Bitting, why do you have a skull on your desk?" To which I would respond by quoting Sirach 7:36, "In whatever you do, remember your last days, and you will never sin." I would tell them about the Latin phrase *memento mori* (remember your death) and tell them stories of saints who are frequently depicted with skulls on their desks as a constant reminder of their death and motivation to avoid sin. More and more students would ask me about the skull. Even students who were not in my classes, walking down the hallway after school would peer in, do a double take and enter my room to ask me about the skull.

There are many ways to provoke curiosity. Perhaps we can write a compelling question on the board, as one of my former students did, before everyone took their seats. "Does God really answer all of our prayers?" Or, we might help them puzzle over a work of art that is relevant to that day's teaching. For instance, what important questions could we help them to raise concerning the extent to which God respects our freedom as we examine Vermeer's *Woman Holding a Balance* or Bosch's *Death and the Miser* or Caravaggio's *The Calling of Saint Matthew*? Or perhaps we begin with the story of Saint Maximilian Kolbe stepping forward that day in Auschwitz, offering to take a condemned man's place in the starvation bunker. Such a story raises the question: What am I willing to die for?

If we adopt this approach of first provoking curiosity, we open up many new possibilities, if even a quarter of participants have become curious before we begin teaching. An atmosphere set apart from the ordinary; strong personal connections; and curious participants are each important. Each leads to the high point of this movement of preparation: our prayerful encounter with God.

OPENING IN PRAYER: EXTRAORDINARY POSSIBILITIES

Leading a prayer can be perfunctory, a purely external exercise. To avoid this, it is helpful here to ask, why do we pray before we teach? Let's consider two important reasons.

First, we pray in order to become attuned to God, who will speak as his word is proclaimed and pondered. Jesus promised that his steadying influence would remain after he ascended into heaven. He assures us that "where two or three are gathered together in my name, there am I in the midst of them" (Mt 18:20). And, when he entrusted his disciples with the Great Commission, he explicitly promised to be accessible to all those throughout the centuries who would strive to accomplish this great work: "I am with you always, until the end of the age" (Mt

28:20). He is with us catechists in this work! Becoming confident in this presence helps us teach from a place of hope.

Yet, his presence is not enough; something more is needed. If we take some time to help those gathered (including ourselves) to become aware of and attuned to his presence, miracles then become possible in the classroom. This is so, even in the most challenging of circumstances, because Christ is present any time the word is proclaimed. It is imperative that those we teach come to experience prayer as Saint Thérèse of Lisieux famously described it, as "a surge of the heart."[5] What would it take for our prayer within the catechetical setting to be a real opportunity for encounter?

Catechists might consider beginning prayer time with some words of encouragement (or gentle exhortation) to turn our interior focus toward God, to be confident that he is present and wants to meet us. However we pray with our students, moments of silence will be pivotal for reflection and their interior movement toward God, particularly before and after Scripture is read. Without these moments, it can be easy to tune out, to remain uninvested. In addition to silence, we might also consider how we cultivate a responsiveness to God in prayer, whether we give them chances to enter into prayerful dialog through music or in some other way. If prayer is an exchange of love, we must allow real opportunities for listening and for giving.

A second reason to pray well at the start of catechesis is this: We catechists have the extraordinary opportunity to not just pray with our learners, but to teach them how to pray. If they live in a home where the family does not pray, their time with us may be the only opportunity they have to learn the art of Christian prayer.

It is to the great good of our students if we understand our-

---

[5] Saint Thérèse of Lisieux, *Manuscrits autobiographiques,* C 25r in CCC 2558.

selves to be guides in the way of Catholic prayer, introducing them to the Catholic spiritual treasury that has supported the growth in holiness of countless of our brothers and sisters through the centuries. We have the chance, through our time with them, to help them become comfortable and confident praying with Scripture, with the liturgy, with music, with silence, with formal prayers, with spontaneous prayer, with Christian prayers from various cultures, with the prayers of the saints, and with the prayer that arises in their own hearts. This requires a spiritual generosity on the part of catechists, to reach beyond our own spiritual preferences and instead open up to them the many avenues of Catholic prayer. Taking this approach will likely introduce them to forms of prayer that will resonate, which they will come to embrace as their own.

My daughter Grace recently went to an amazing Catholic summer camp outside of Columbus, Ohio, where they excel in teaching young people how to pray. Each morning, the kids at camp not only pray together, but they also learn how to pray, mentored every morning in their small groups. Lauren Gothard, Grace's "prayer lab" leader, describes the approach:

> At Catholic Youth Summer Camp, we desire to form young missionary disciples in a way that is sustainable. Camp is only one week, but we want campers to follow Jesus every day of their lives. This is where "prayer lab" comes in. We spend thirty minutes every morning mentoring campers into a personal prayer life through *lectio divina* and teaching them what Jesus' voice sounds like in their lives. We talk about how Matthew 7:7 says, "Ask and it will be given you; seek and you will find; knock and the door will be opened to you." We walk with campers as they begin to ask Jesus "do you love me?" and

"what do you want to say to me?" These basic questions bear incredible fruit. Campers hear Jesus say, in the quiet place of their hearts, "I love you more than all the stars in the sky," and "I want you to follow me." In this way, prayer is no longer a chore or a list of memorized words, but a living relationship. This prayer, grounded in Scripture and the teachings of the Church, is something the campers thirst for. The "mountaintop experience" of camp can be taken home and experienced every day because they know how to meet Jesus in personal prayer.

Teaching prayer empowers young people to not always rely on others to lead them in prayer, but to become people of prayer themselves. When catechesis includes this kind of formation in how to pray, the passivity or awkwardness in prayer at the beginning of the year can grow to become a learned ability as students become more confident in the art of prayer.

And so, in this movement of preparation, we encourage participants to temporarily put their preoccupations to the side. We help them into a place of curiosity and interest in what we will teach them. And finally, we invite them to prayerfully encounter God who so generously makes himself present to us. We are able to do many things ourselves to help the conditions of the soil, but truly encountering God prepares the soil of the heart like nothing else can.

These are the essentials of what we work for in this first movement of catechesis. Imagine the possibilities for each person who chooses to take these steps.

PUTTING "PREPARATION" INTO PRACTICE

Your own life of prayer and sacramental practice (as discussed in chapters 2 and 3) prepares you to lead others to encounter God in his word. How is your own life of communion with God perceptible to your students?

Do you pray on your own before you teach? Are there specific ways in which you offer yourself to the Lord, your teaching, and those whom you are about to teach?

What are the distractions and difficulties that you encounter in your teaching space? What are some first steps you can take to enhance the environment, to help it better reflect the sacredness of catechesis, even if the room is borrowed and not your permanent space?

At the end of each of these next four chapters, we will consider how we could craft each step if we were teaching the doctrine of the angels. If you were planning to teach about angels, what are some concrete, age-appropriate ways that curiosity can be provoked before teaching?

How can you strengthen personal connections between participants? Between them and yourself?

What steps can you take to create opportunities for prayer to be a genuine encounter?

CHAPTER SIX

Proclamation
Planting the Seed

The soil has been cultivated and carefully prepared. We are ready now for the most significant step: the planting of the seed. Just as it is with most gardeners, so it is with us catechists: The seedling that we plant in the soil of the heart is not our own creation; it has its origins in God. As master catechists Barbara Morgan and Sister Athanasius Munroe, OP, explain, "God wishes to speak to us as friends, to invite us to share in his life. This shocking and wonderful reality exceeds anything we could ever imagine on our own; we must be told it."[1]

---

[1] Barbara Morgan and Sister Athanasius Munroe, OP, *Echoing the Mystery: Unlocking the Deposit of Faith in Catechesis* (Ann Arbor, MI: Lumen Ecclesiae Press, 2018), 12.

The catechist, then, puts herself alongside Saint Paul, who reveals to others something of immeasurable value, something that he himself first had to receive: "For I handed on to you as of first importance what I also received: that Christ died for our sins in accordance with the scriptures" (1 Cor 15:3). We catechists hand on to our students what we have first received from God: his word, his teaching, the Good News of his invitation to share in his life. Each human being depends on others to be told the content of the Gospel, which illumines for every person the real trajectory of life and of our true homeland.

Here, though, is an important question for us catechists: How do we offer the precious content of the Gospel in such a way that it might be received as a great treasure, as the "pearl of great price," which a person sells all that he has in order to attain? (Mt 13:46) To answer this question, we first observe the One whose words and methods must form our own teaching.

THE ORIGINS OF
CHRISTIAN PROCLAMATION

Reading through the New Testament, paying close attention to how Jesus and then his disciples taught, reveals a defining characteristic: The teaching of Christ and the saving events of his life, death, and resurrection were understood to be "Good News." His words and deeds were not just explained. They were announced. Indeed, they were ardently proclaimed.

Our Lord's teaching was filled with bold, stirring proclamations. The exhortations we see in the Gospels are truth statements that could just as well end with exclamation points as periods. Here are just a few examples:

- "I am the way and the truth and the life. No one comes to the Father except through me" (Jn 14:6).

- "Ask and it will be given to you; seek and you will find; knock and the door will be opened to you" (Mt 7:7).
- "For God so loved the world that he gave his only Son, so that everyone who believes in him might not perish but might have eternal life" (Jn 3:16).

And we should not forget those exhortations of his that were contentious and sharply critical of the religious leaders of his time. Here are a few instances:

- "Let the one among you who is without sin be the first to throw a stone at her" (Jn 8:7).
- "Woe to you, scribes and Pharisees, you hypocrites. You are like whitewashed tombs, which appear beautiful on the outside, but inside are full of dead men's bones and every kind of filth" (Mt 23:27).
- "It is written, 'My house shall be a house of prayer, but you have made it a den of thieves'" (Lk 19:46).

Our Lord's teaching was not bland. It did not promote passivity. Rather, it was exhortative, stirring up a responsiveness in those who heard him teach. C. S. Lewis famously pointed out that Our Lord was either Lord, liar, or lunatic, which means it is not possible to remain neutral to Christ.[2] If this is true, then this quality about him that compelled a choice is ever present in his teaching. And we see, therefore, a tendency to respond to Christ in many of the men and women we meet in the Gospels.

---

[2] See C. S. Lewis, *Mere Christianity* (London: Collins, 1952), 54–56.

We might remember here the backlash in Nazareth the first time the people in Jesus' native place heard him teach. His words "filled [them] with fury. They rose up, drove him out of the town, and led him to the brow of the hill on which their town had been built, to hurl him down headlong" (Lk 4:28–29). Could there have been a more dramatic — and troubling — homecoming for Jesus of Nazareth? We also meet the rich young man who "went away sad, for he had many possessions" (Mt 19:22). The Lord challenged him to "sell what you have and give to [the] poor, and you will have treasure in heaven. Then come, follow me" (Mt 19:21). Faced with the invitation to radical discipleship, the young man was unwilling to pay such a price. We can also recall the crowds who, upon hearing Jesus say "whoever eats my flesh and drinks my blood remains in me and I in him" responded by simply walking away. "This saying is hard; who can accept it?" (cf. Jn 6:35–60).

Of course, Jesus' exhortative way of teaching also brought about many favorable responses from those who heard him. We read, for instance, of Simon Peter's response of faith to Our Lord's question, "But who do you say that I am?" Peter responded, "You are the Messiah, the Son of the living God" (Mt 16:15–16). In another place, we read that "the crowds were astonished at his teaching, for he taught them as one having authority, and not as their scribes" (Mt 7:28–29). And, on the road to Emmaus, the Lord's two disciples responded to his gentle rebuke ("Oh, how foolish you are! How slow of heart to believe all that the prophets spoke!") and subsequent teaching by asking this mysterious Visitor to stay with them, "for it is nearly evening and the day is almost over" (cf. Lk 24:13–35).

The point? Jesus' words had power. They were provocative. He proclaimed. He exhorted. He challenged. His words vividly stand out and stick in the memory. Jesus spoke the truth with boldness, in a way that evoked a reply — one way or the other —

from each of his hearers.

After Our Lord ascended into heaven, the Gospel was boldly proclaimed by the early Christians who also understood the
challenging, life-altering nature of Christ's words and his deeds.
The saving events of his suffering, death, resurrection, and as-
cension into heaven — and his promise to come again — formed
the content of the Church's proclamation to the world. For these
early disciples, the Good News had its center in the extraordinary tidings of the empty tomb. Peter Kreeft and Father Ronald
Tacelli explain this important characteristic mark of the early
Christians' message: "Every sermon preached by every Christian
in the New Testament centers on the resurrection. The gospel or
'good news' means essentially the news of Christ's resurrection.
The message that flashed across the ancient world, set hearts on
fire, changed lives and turned the world upside down was not
'love your neighbor.' Every morally sane person already knew
that; it was not news. The news was that a man who claimed to
be the Son of God and the Savior of the world had risen from
the dead."[3]

The Gospel, the astonishing announcement of the God-Man
who has risen from the dead, burst upon the world through the
bold testimony of real witnesses to these events. They were propelled to share this news of Christ's victory over sin and death
throughout the Roman empire and beyond. If Jesus rose from
the dead, then his words and deeds are true and supremely important, and they were announced as such. His words are for all
people of all times, because they are the words of God incarnate.
"Woe to me if I do not preach [the Gospel]," writes Paul (1 Cor
9:16). This instinct for proclamation, so clearly evident in the
person of Jesus, animated the early Church, filled as it was with

---

[3] Peter Kreeft and Ronald K. Tacelli, *Handbook of Christian Apologetics* (Downers Grove, IL: Inter-
Varsity Press, 1994), 176.

the missionary zeal of the Holy Spirit.

The early Christians went out to the world with this message because this is what Jesus himself told them they must do. His last recorded words to them (in the Gospel of Mark) make this clear: "Go into the whole world and proclaim the gospel to every creature. Whoever believes and is baptized will be saved; whoever does not believe will be condemned" (Mk 16:15–16). And so, from the very early years, Christians announced. They proclaimed. They understood this work of proclamation to have life-or-death consequences for those to whom they spoke. The content of the Christian message, then, was unlike anything else they could give to people, because it is the revealed Word of the Creator and Savior of the world.

OUR NEED FOR THE GOSPEL

It is this same word — preserved and proclaimed for the last twenty centuries by the Church, in a process guided and inspired by the Holy Spirit — that we pass on today through our catechesis. But how should we carry out this vitally important responsibility?

When we teach in the way we see modeled in the Gospels and the whole of the New Testament, our teaching will also rouse the hearts and minds of those we teach. Because the content of our teaching is the content of the Gospel, which belongs to Christ, our teaching contains an inherent power and authority. It is vital today (and in every age) that the content of the Faith be proclaimed in its newness and power. If, instead of boldly proclaiming, we are only explaining, elaborating, questioning, and applying, then our methods are not aligned with the true nature of what we teach. The teachings of Christ and of his Church are true and so extraordinarily beautiful and good. They come from God, and they contain the call to repentance that will bring us into the fullness of life and joy. Therefore, they must include the characteristic mark of proclamation if catechesis is to be a true echoing down of the glad tidings of Christ.

Father Tom Forrest, CSsR, puts it this way: "There is nothing more natural than wanting to share the Good News. When a man wins a million-dollar lottery, he almost falls from the window in his excitement to share that news with a neighbor. Jesus himself talks about shouting not from a window but from the housetops, shouting the Good News about all he has won for us by his cross (see Matthew 10:27). On another occasion he says that if Christians stayed silent with this kind of Good News, 'the very stones would cry out' (Luke 19:40)."[4]

Proclaiming the content of the Gospel does justice to God's Word and its original mode of delivery. Yet it also corresponds to a great need present in each person, a need to receive the Word of God as the Good News for me. For Magdalena Gutierrez of Hyattsville, Maryland, the first time she heard the message of Christ proclaimed in a stirring way — and specifically, his call to evangelize — the experience was unforgettable.

> When I was in seventh grade growing up in Monterrey, Mexico, a young priest came to my Catholic school and gave a homily on evangelization. In earlier years, I had been taught that God created and loved me. I had heard many stories from salvation history. I had been told about the sacraments and the need to pray. But this was the first time I had ever heard proclaimed with passion that every baptized person was called to evangelize. This meant that I, personally, had this call from God. This priest explained that I was called and even qualified for this because of the grace of

---

[4] Father Tom Forrest, CSsR, "Why Should Catholics Evangelize?" in Ralph Martin and Peter Williamson, eds., *John Paul II and the New Evangelization: How You Can Bring the Good News to Others* (Cincinnati, OH: Servant Books, 2006), 35.

God already given to me in baptism. In my heart,
I knew this was for me. I knew that I wanted to
be part of the mission, this great work. And I remember saying to myself, "Are you ready? Let's
go! I want to do this!"

Because of that homily and that proclamation of that truth, every time I heard the word
"evangelization" I paid attention. I continued
to learn and grow and say "yes!" In these years
since, I've come to understand that when the
truth is proclaimed as Good News and includes
an invitation to embrace it, the Holy Spirit is already there in the heart of the baptized, helping
us to respond, to say "yes," to move with it. But,
we have to have the chance to say, "Yes, I'm in!"

We might recall from chapter 4 that the Church's announcement
to the world contains two vital elements, just as Christ's teaching
did: the proclamation of Good News and the call to conversion.
Magdalena's experience illustrates both of these elements: Her
heart was stirred by the call to evangelize, and she understood
clearly that she was being personally challenged to live in a new
way. It was important to accept the Good News, but it was also
necessary to respond to it, to step forward.

Jason Evert offers us a compelling illustration of how the
Good News about love and sexuality (even though it wasn't
framed from a Catholic perspective) set into motion a significant change in a young woman who heard him speak:

After giving a chastity talk at a public high school
in Texas, an older teenage girl approached me
and was noticeably upset. She confided in me
that she left her parents several months ago and

eloped with an older man. The two married in Las Vegas, and were living together in a tumultuous relationship. Speaking at length about his violent temper and drug problems, she rolled up her sleeves and showed me the bruises in the shape of his hands, where he had grabbed her during an argument. They had been fighting about her recent miscarriage of her twins. He blamed her for the loss because when she was a child, she had been sexually abused and contracted an STD that required aggressive surgery to treat. As a result of the procedure, she suffered from cervical incompetence, meaning that she would have difficulty maintaining a full-term pregnancy.

Standing before this poor young woman, I thought to myself, "What can I possibly say to begin undoing all the hurt she's experienced?" I asked, "What's your dream? Where do you want to be in ten years?" Her eyes brightened, and she replied, "I want to go to New York City and be a Broadway dancer." "Great!" I responded. "What are you doing to get there?" She looked down and said that she had received a scholarship to NYU, but her husband wouldn't let her leave Texas. We began strategizing ways for her to return to her family, and I explained how we needed to report what was happening in her relationship.

Soon, she was living at home with her parents again and emailed me to tell how her ex-husband threw rocks up at her bedroom window, yelling for her to return to him. But she didn't. More than a year later, I received an

email from a joy-filled college girl in New York
City who was flourishing in the NYU dance
program. She added that she also found a great
Catholic guy who would soon be flying home
with her for Thanksgiving break so that he
could meet her family.

When this same young woman had walked
into her high school auditorium to hear a chastity talk, there's little chance that she expected
to hear good news. Odds are, she expected fear
tactics, shame, condemnation, and a litany of
prohibitions. Although it was a public school
and nothing religious was mentioned, she still
discovered the way to live, the truth about love,
and the life she deserved. She encountered
Christ without hearing his name. She realized
that she was created for authentic human love,
and nothing less would ever satisfy her.

Like the early Christians and the saints, each of us needs to hear
the truth of Christ announced boldly as the Good News that it
is. We must perceive in the Gospel a challenge to a new way of
living. Each of us must come to see that the content of Christianity comes from God and has divine authority (because it is true),
and therefore is a secure foundation around which to base our
life and view of the world. The content of the Faith is thus only
rightly understood when it is perceived to be the bold, joyful announcement that it is. If we see the Catholic Faith merely as a set
of propositions to be explained and studied, we are missing its
fundamental quality. The Faith proclaimed, on the other hand,
challenges us, provokes with us a desire to respond, and moves
us to take steps forward.

This movement of proclamation recovers within catechesis

that instinct of the early Christians — and of Christ himself —
to courageously announce these glad tidings as objectively true,
good, and beautiful, meant for every human being. This desire
to proclaim Christ and to call people to conversion springs naturally from our own transforming encounter with him. The great
saints, of course, show this. Take, for instance, Saint Francis of
Assisi. His own intimate communion with the Lord filled him
with such zeal and joy that he could not contain the Good News
within himself. It had to be shared. One author imaginatively
describes the young Francis's generosity of spirit and his sense of
being a herald of the Great King:

> Francis spoke to everyone who gave him a
> friendly nod. He met a farmer and talked with
> him about cattle and about God. He stood and
> talked with a charwoman about her children
> and about the sorrows of the Blessed Virgin.
> The woman listened, with the duster in her
> hand, as though he were telling her some sad
> but important news. A little later he was sitting
> on some alley steps telling a swarm of dirty ur-
> chins about the stable of Bethlehem. When he
> got back to the Portiuncula that evening, his
> hunger reminded him that he had forgotten
> to beg. "Brother Ass," he said to his body, "just
> keep quiet a while, little fellow. Tomorrow I'll
> make the rounds and get you something to eat!"
> And Brother Ass kept quiet.[5]

The proclamation of the Good News permeated Francis's words

---

[5] Felix Timmermans, *The Perfect Joy of Saint Francis*, trans. L. A. Aspelagh (San Francisco: Ignatius Press, 1998), 81–82.

and actions, bringing tremendous renewal to the Church and the world. The word proclaimed and lived has that kind of power.

STEPS FORWARD FOR THE CATECHIST

How do we as catechists proclaim within teaching? Rest assured, this does not require that you raise the pitch of your voice, stand on a chair, or adopt a preachy approach to your students. Rather, there are realistic ways to recover not only the practice of proclamation but also the conviction that what we proclaim and teach comes from God, and therefore has its own inner power to change us.

James Bitting of Wichita, Kansas, made a surprising discovery in his high school classroom a few years back:

> When I began teaching, I tended to summarize
> Scripture passages in my own words rather than
> taking the extra time to open up my Bible and
> proclaim the passage. At some point I started
> to feel guilty about this. I recalled Pope Saint
> Paul VI's words that conversion occurs, "solely
> through the divine power of the message [the
> Church] proclaims." I decided that even though
> it was going to take more time, whenever I re-
> ferred to a Scripture passage in class, rather
> than paraphrasing, I would open my Bible and
> read it to my students. I noticed a change in my
> students' attentiveness and behavior almost im-
> mediately. In the past, when I would paraphrase
> a Scripture passage, some students seemed dis-
> interested and some talked to classmates while
> I was teaching. But when I started reading di-
> rectly from Scripture, the students became
> much more attentive and behavior problems

decreased. I did not make any changes to my discipline methods that could explain their sudden and persistent improvement in behavior. The only change I made was reading directly from the Bible rather than paraphrasing.

For example, instead of simply saying, "the Jews were severely persecuted by the Greeks but a small remnant remained faithful even under torture and death," I would read 2 Maccabees 7. You could hear a pin drop, they were so attentive! Instead of saying, "Jesus said this or that," I would open the Gospels and read aloud. I started seeing the power of the proclaimed word in action. Students became more interested, and they asked more questions. Sacred Scripture began to engage their reason and touch their heart in ways that my words could not do.

James's experience confirms what we all know conceptually: The word of God has its own inherent power. Scripture is indeed "living and effective, sharper than any two-edged sword, penetrating even between soul and spirit, joints and marrow, and able to discern reflections and thoughts of the heart" (Heb 4:12). Featuring it prominently, allowing it to be the driving force for what we teach, invests catechesis with a divine power for helping people perceive the voice of God. Our words are just not the same, eloquent and convincing as we try to be.

In addition to relying on Sacred Scripture, there is another strategy by which we can recover the dynamic of proclamation in our teaching. We could adopt a phrase or a sentence or a couple of sentences from either Sacred Scripture or Sacred Tradition, something that could serve as the foundation for that day's catechesis, and make it the reverberating touchstone of a particular lesson. Just as we easily recall certain phrases of Our Lord on account of their sticking power, we can amplify a profound expression of truth in such a way that it stands out as the most important of the catechesis. How might a catechist do this? At the beginning of the lesson, the catechist should first proclaim the most essential truth of the catechesis. This proclamation would then be situated in the central position of the catechesis and would be (we hope!) the primary words echoing in the minds and imaginations of the students as they leave the session. Teaching in this way sets these particular words as the hub of the wheel, with primary teaching points being as closely connected as spokes to the hub of the wheel.

Apologist and writer Frank Sheed provides us an example of just such an approach. In the following excerpt from his very helpful little book *Are We Really Teaching Religion?*, pay attention to what he proclaims and how he then teaches from this proclamation. Sheed writes, "Catholicism means the union of men with God in Christ. That is Catholicism, that is all of Catholicism. That is the fact they should have standing up clear and clean from all the mass of things they know." We may note here the hint of mystery present within these sentences. Beginning with a sentence that draws attention to the reality of union (a concept with which many Catholics in Sheed's time, and still today, would not be familiar), Sheed doubles down and asserts that this is the idea — above all others — that Catholic young people most need to understand. He continues:

> As they come through school, they have learnt
> a great number of things, but there is no order,
> no hierarchy, in the things they have learnt about
> the faith. They have all sorts of pious practices,
> good salutary practices, rubbing shoulders, so to
> speak, with essentials. They hardly know which

is which, they are all there together in a kind of
— I was going to say rag bag, but that would be
rude — they are all there in a kind of heap. The
absolutely essential activities of Catholicism and
the quite desirable but non-essential pious practices — all there together — the Trinity hardly
larger than Our Lady of Fatima! They need some
framework on which they can arrange their
knowledge, to which all the rest can be related.

The union of men with God in Christ is Catholicism; and, that being so, whatever else they
are clear or vague about, whatever else they remember or do not remember, they should be
absolutely clear on *what God is, what man is,
what Christ is, what union is.* Those four should
stand out like a great plateau — you can arrange
all the other things around these.[6]

For Sheed, the content of his proclamation ("Catholicism is the
union of men with God in Christ") comes into clearer focus as
each of the four pillars of this truth statement is better understood. And this is no bland statement around which he centers
his teaching. This truth about Catholicism is bold, winsome, and
worthy of being announced from the rooftops!

Following Sheed's lead, then, how might we incorporate a
similar strategy? Two things are important here: where we find a
proclamation, and how we use it.

First, the proclamation needs to be identified.
Whatever we select, this phrase or short passage must be foun-

---

[6] Frank Sheed, *Are We Really Teaching Religion?* (New York: Sheed and Ward Inc., 1953), 14 (emphasis original).

dational to all else that will be taught.[7] Rather than choosing something somewhat peripheral (On the fifth day, "God created the great sea monsters" [Gn 1:21]), we're aiming for a suitable footing for the whole catechesis (God creates and finds his creation very good [cf. Gn 1:31]).

Our proclamation could be drawn directly from Sacred Scripture. In fact, proclamation is the natural and appropriate habitat for Sacred Scripture within catechesis, since Scripture is meant to be announced and proclaimed. Here are some biblical examples:

- "Whoever wishes to come after me must deny himself, take up his cross, and follow me." (Mt 16:24)
- "What profit is there for one to gain the whole world and forfeit his life?" (Mk 8:36)
- "For I am convinced that neither death, nor life, nor angels, nor principalities, nor present things, nor future things, nor powers, nor height, nor depth, nor any other creature will be able to separate us from the love of God in Christ Jesus our Lord." (Rom 8:38–39)
- "God is love, and whoever remains in love remains in God and God in him." (1 Jn 4:16)

Our proclamation could also be drawn from Sacred Tradition, as this, too, is a life-giving channel of God's revelation:

---

[7] When it comes to identifying the foundation for the various doctrinal teachings that make up the Church's Faith, a marvelous new book sets out what it calls "the divine perspective" and the essential dimensions that ought to be covered for each of the Church's primary doctrines. This book is very helpful to the task of preparing catecheses that do justice to the depth and breadth of the Deposit of Revelation. See Barbara Morgan and Sister Athanasius Munroe, OP, *Echoing the Mystery: Unlocking the Deposit of Faith in Catechesis* (Ann Arbor, MI: Lumen Ecclesiae Press, 2018).

- "Behold the wood of the Cross, on which is hung our salvation! Come, let us adore!" (Good Friday Liturgy)
- "The glory of God is the human being fully alive." (Saint Irenaeus)
- "The value of one person transcends all the material world." (Saint John Paul II)
- "O happy fault, O necessary sin of Adam, which gained for us so great a Redeemer!" (Exsultet, Easter Vigil)

As a still valuable third option, the catechist himself could sometimes create his own proclamation, tailored to the specific content and audience being taught. A few years ago, our associate pastor began his homily with these words: "I am third." The Gospel that day was drawn from Luke 10 and focused on the greatest commandment: "You shall love the Lord, your God, with all your heart, with all your being, with all your strength, and with all your mind, and your neighbor as yourself." As he described this ordering of human love and the importance of putting God and others before ourselves, he kept coming back to his pithy — yet memorable — proclamation: "I am third." In doing this, Father Tyron gave us something to hold on to, a hook in our memories on which the Great Commandment was able to hang and be remembered. Later that Sunday afternoon, our youngest daughters Mairen and Monica surprised us with an evocative drawing with "I am third" in the center. We attached this to the refrigerator for a couple of weeks and kept talking about it and trying to live this challenging maxim. To this day, every member of our family remembers that three-word sentence. It has retained its power.

We could identify a few helpful characteristics for any effective proclamation within catechesis:

- It should be God-centered. A good proclamation will be clearly oriented to God: from him, about him, leading us toward him. This is why the words of Scripture are particularly powerful to employ in catechesis in this way. If God-centered, it is its orientation to God that gives it its immense potential to move us deeply, putting us into contact with God's way of seeing.

- It should be interesting and challenging. A proclamation that is stale, below (or above) our developmental level, dry, or boring is counterproductive. Nothing induces passivity and indifference more quickly. Because of this, a definition rarely makes for a good proclamation, as the sentence structure of a definition doesn't typically captivate. Instead, proclamations that bring us into contact with the mysterious quality of the Faith are the best choices. We hope here for another provocation by the power, beauty, goodness, and compelling wonder of the Truth.

- Finally (as can be seen in the earlier examples), a good proclamation is short, concise, and easy to remember. Above all the other content they receive during the catechesis, we want these words to stand out, to be the one thing ringing in their ears as they leave the catechetical setting. Therefore, it needs to be memorable, able to be treasured as Good News of dignity and power that students want to retain for themselves.

If a phrase or a sentence or a few sentences together meet these criteria, there is a good chance it will be helpful to us in this movement of proclamation. Matthew Maxwell of St. Louis, Missouri, shares this story of employing just such a proclamation in his youth ministry:

> It is challenging to proclaim objective truth in the midst of a world that doesn't want to commit the time to understanding or processing truth. Apply this to my work with teenagers in youth ministry and the proclamation of objective truth becomes even more daunting! To this end, I have always found the idea of "proclamation" to be valuable and have never skimped on its integration into any of our youth nights. It is important in today's bit-sized, short-attention span society to be able to distill a complex concept of the Faith into its most necessary focus so as to make it more palatable and winsome to those with whom we are sharing the Gospel.
>
> A few years back we held a youth group night shortly before Valentine's Day, focusing on the model of Christ's love as the basis for authentic relationships. I spoke briefly on the intersection of Valentine's Day and the need to recapture a true sense of what it means to love another. After this brief two-minute summary of the night's topic of discussion, I shared with them the night's proclamation from Saint Maximilian Kolbe: "The Cross is the school of love." I also created a nice-looking graphic of the quote and projected it on the wall.
>
> A couple months later, I was meeting with one of our young men who was discerning the seminary. Amongst other topics of conversation,

we talked about the love and sacrifice necessary to be a priest, at which point he proclaimed
back to me, "The Cross is the school of love." He
then proceeded to tell me how that quote from
Maximilian Kolbe had remained with him from
months earlier, and will remain an important
maxim for him. He is now in his second year of
seminary formation.

Second, we take steps to allow the proclamation to have its full influence and power.

Once we've located or crafted a good proclamation, what do we do
with it? The following three strategies will be particularly helpful.

- First, the proclamation is reinforced at key moments throughout the catechesis. As we teach
  the content of our lesson, we frequently come
  back to the proclamation, which is the lesson's
  broader context. Because the proclamation is a
  foundational truth for the lesson, as we teach,
  the proclamation will become more clear, more
  vivid, more likely to be understood and embraced. This kind of reinforcement increases
  the chance that the essentials of our catechesis
  will be remembered.

- Second, we will want to make sure our proclamation is visually present in some way in the learning space. In my first year teaching catechetics
  students, as my students were giving critiqued
  presentations, the first student wrote her proclamation up on the chalkboard. The second student upped the effectiveness factor and wrote

a lot on the board as he taught, but used green chalk for the proclamation, helping it to stand out. A third student moved away from simple chalk and put her proclamation up on colorful poster board, which made it stand out all the more. I've seen proclamations printed out nicely and put in a frame and set up within the prayer space to accent their importance and beauty. I've seen proclamations featured prominently in video presentations, on handouts, and even folded up and placed within plastic Easter eggs. There are so many creative ways to make proclamations visually accessible to different age groups.

The movement of proclamation is the shortest movement of an evangelizing catechesis, but it is the most significant. Whether we conceive of proclamation as the second step of a teaching method or incorporate it in some other way, the content of Christianity must be announced as Good News. With this announcement comes the possibility that our students will encounter our teaching for what it is: inspired by the revealed word of God, full of potential to challenge and change us. Proclamation changes the tone of catechesis from merely expository to exhortative. And as proclamation becomes integral to our teaching, we will more closely resemble Christ the Teacher. The next steps of our catechesis then naturally follow from this proclamation, for we must seek to understand and eventually respond to the Good News that has been proclaimed.

PUTTING "PROCLAMATION" INTO PRACTICE

It's helpful to put these principles right into practice.

Before we choose a proclamation, it is important to understand the central truth about a doctrine that will be reflected in the proclamation. For this exercise, we will use the same sample topic of angels that was mentioned in chapter 5. Carefully read the *Catechism* paragraphs on angels (CCC 328–36), looking for the main point that sums up what we need to know about angels. You can also engage sources such as Scripture, the liturgy, the saints, and (if applicable) your textbook. Consider looking at the relevant section in the *Catechism* and locate the Scripture references given in the footnotes. These Scriptures will be important to your own study and teaching. This central point should reflect the Good News in a hopeful manner. Be sure to keep the students you serve in mind as you develop your proclamation.

Find a phrase or sentence that could be used. Be sure that this proclamation reflects a central element of the doctrine and is something you can make your own and proclaim from your heart. As a final takeaway, consider especially these four qualities of a compelling proclamation suggested in this chapter: 1) God-centered; 2) interesting; 3) short and easy to remember; and 4) given from the heart. Each of these is important to identifying and crafting a winsome proclamation.

CHAPTER SEVEN

Explanation
Helping the Plant to Grow

Every living thing needs nourishment. When the seedling is put into the earth, we pack it in with good soil and provide plenty of water. We continue to water it and protect it. We do just enough so that it receives the light it needs (which is provided by God), with the hope that the seedling "takes" in its new home and is able to grow on its own.

In catechesis, what we proclaim now needs to be nourished and developed so that it, too, can grow. The question of the Ethiopian in the Acts of the Apostles ought to resonate with us: "How can I [understand] unless someone instructs me?" (8:31). Indeed, the content of the Good News, which comes from God himself, is suffused with mystery, beauty, depth upon depth. It needs to be explained.

Keep in mind here our convictions regarding catechesis and missionary discipleship. For those who are skeptical of the idea that catechesis today can engage people (let alone evangelize them and contribute to their formation as missionary disciples), this is the step that will be most worrisome. Of course, for some of us, it was during the detailed explanations in the catechesis of our early years that we became most passive and lost interest. Others received a catechesis of little substance, yet with similar results. For many of today's parents, the uninteresting catechesis they experienced as children is an important reason why they undervalue catechesis for their own little ones.

The first two movements of catechesis (explored in the last two chapters) are important steps forward, but now we have to ask this important question: Is it possible to explain the Faith in ways that will keep participants interested, inspiring them to grow to be disciples? Unequivocally, yes! But much will hinge on their experience of how the content is communicated.

There are two overarching priorities that, when respected, increase the likelihood that we can teach in a transformative way. The first has to do with how we see the content of our lesson. The second concerns our approach to the people who sit before us. First, we must be faithful to God and the content of his revelation; at the same time, without in any way diminishing the content of what we teach, we must be faithful to the learning capacities of those we teach. Neither of these sacred responsibilities may be compromised. When it comes to our methods of teaching, Saint John Paul II insisted that we are to serve both revelation and conversion.[1] Our catechesis must reverence the word of God, which becomes the transforming power of our teaching. Concurrently, we must work for the high objective of

---

[1] See John Paul II, *Catechesi Tradendae,* accessed April 20, 2020, Vatican.va, par. 52.

helping our students grow to truly become disciples.

CATECHESIS FOR THE CHRISTIAN MESSAGE

What we teach is something infinitely profound. It has been entrusted by God to the Church, that it might be clearly communicated to people of every time. It is important to keep before us the divine origin of the content of catechesis. Thus, our primary source for our catechesis must be Divine Revelation; that is, Sacred Scripture and Sacred Tradition as it is authentically interpreted by the Magisterium of the Church. We must continually form ourselves in this revealed word so that we ourselves might be transformed by the renewal of our minds (cf. Rom 12:2). This is the first way we reverence God's word in our capacity as catechists: by continuing to prayerfully study what God has revealed. Then, God's word will not be dry content for us, but a living, dynamic word that we have made central to how we think and pray and live — to the great good of those we teach.

The content of our teaching, then, is not our own. It has been entrusted to us by God through the Church. Rooted in God's Revelation and prayerfully attuned to Christ present in this sacred place, as our students hear us teach, it will be Christ himself who teaches. For us catechists, uniting our own initiative to the movement of divine grace as we teach is a great mystery. Children's catechist Sofia Cavalletti puts it this way: "At times our hands touch the presence of an active force that is not ours, and it is precisely because it is not our own that it fills us with wonder and deep joy."[2] Reverencing the content of Revelation that has been entrusted to us by the Church makes us instruments in the hand of Christ the Teacher.

Deep convictions will arise for people of all ages when Sa-

---

[2] Sofia Cavalletti, *The Religious Potential of the Child* (Chicago: Catechesis of the Good Shepherd Publications, 1992), 52.

cred Scripture is reverently pondered and placed at the center of catechesis. We must draw on Sacred Tradition, too. The *Catechism of the Catholic Church* is the best expression of this deposit of Sacred Tradition in our contemporary day. We also have access to the Tradition in the signs, symbols, and prayers of the Sacred Liturgy as it has developed over the centuries; in the writings of the saints; and in the authoritative teaching of the Magisterium. When we root ourselves in God's word, our teaching will become enlivened by an attractiveness and a boldness that is not our own. And it will have tremendous power to change us and those we teach.

Seeing the preeminence of the word of God for catechesis, how can we be attentive to its right position within the practicalities of our own teaching? Here are five ways to get started.

- In planning a lesson, first turn to what God has revealed. Catechists can turn to many sources in preparing to teach: a textbook, a program, supplementary videos, or our own experiences of Catholic faith and life. Important and helpful as these are, we must first sit with God's word ourselves, prayerfully considering its meaning. We can easily fall into the habit of relying on others' interpretations, as so many prepackaged, expertly planned lessons are available today. We must, as disciples ourselves, first immerse ourselves in the content of Sacred Scripture and Sacred Tradition, so that we can speak from God's word as convicted witnesses. An excellent place to dive in is with the relevant sections in the *Catechism,* along with the Scriptures cited in the footnotes. Such study helps us to grasp the essentials and opens us to God's way of seeing the content of our catechesis.

- In the classroom, reverence the Bible as a sacred text. It's important not to leave the Bible under a stack of books or a coffee cup. If we want them to recognize this book as different from all others, we have to show them. Perhaps we open the Bible before they come in and put it in a place of prominence. If we open the Bible to read during prayer, consider lighting a candle as a sign that we are going to receive God's own word, which is "a lamp for my feet, a light for my path" (Ps 119:105). We could also stand as the Gospel is proclaimed and communally respond, "Praise to you, Lord Jesus Christ!"

- Bear witness to the word of God in our teaching and in our body language. I won't forget the older gentleman who was my eighth-grade parish catechist. His love for the Bible — and his reliance on it in teaching — was striking to me. He would teach and answer questions by opening his Bible. And he even smiled as he looked up passages! He was the first person to share with me the famous words of Saint Jerome, that "ignorance of Scripture is ignorance of Christ." It was clear and obvious to me that this was a man who loved the word of God, found encouragement and direction in these pages, and tried very hard to center his life on the content of God's word. I had never met anyone quite like him. And even though at that stage in my spiritual development I did not let on that I was intrigued by this witness, I was.

His reverence for Scripture planted seeds in me that later would come to fruition.

- Incorporate Sacred Scripture and Sacred Tradition prudentially as we teach. It's much better to spend time absorbed in two or three Scripture passages, rather than to try and fit in eight or ten. A large number of scriptural references can sap curiosity, whereas spending time immersing learners in, for example, the vision of the last judgment seen in Matthew 25, helps us to wonder with the text. Sacred Tradition, too, should be drawn upon; but again, not with a flurry of excerpts. The *Catechism of the Catholic Church* is far from a mere doctrinal reference book; rather, it is a beautiful synthesis of the Christian Faith and life, drawn together in its symphonic unity. Elizabeth Siegel writes:

> The *Catechism* is a powerful instrument of formation because it expresses so clearly and so beautifully the truths of the Christian mysteries, and their interconnection with one another. Each doctrine is seen in relation to the central truths of the Trinity, the Paschal Mystery, the Church, and the dignity of the human person. Each doctrine is presented through its foundations in Sacred Scripture — with its power to penetrate minds and hearts, and through its sources in the Tradition, as expressed in the Church fathers and

doctors, the councils, and the saints.[3]

- Help participants to treasure the word of God
  in their heart. Saint John Paul II put it very well
  when he wrote: "The blossoms, if we may call
  them that, of faith and piety do not grow in the
  desert places of a memory-less catechesis."[4] Remembering the content of the Faith, keeping it
  "in the heart," represents a much deeper possession of God's word than pulling it up instan-
  taneously on a screen. It puts the memory to
  use for the very highest purpose. And, as the
  Psalmist reminds us, keeping God's word in our
  heart opens the way to a holy life, a life of virtue:

> How can the young keep his way with
>   out fault?
> Only by observing your words.
> With all my heart I seek you;
>   do not let me stray from your com-
>   mandments.
> In my heart I treasure your promise,
>   that I may not sin against you. ...
> I will ponder your precepts
>   and consider your paths.
> In your statutes I take delight;
>   I will never forget your word.
>   (Ps 119:9–11, 15–16)

Aware of the problems with the memorization methods of cat-

---

[3] Elizabeth Siegel, "Opening the Treasures of the Church: The Catechism in Adult Faith Formation," *The Catechetical Review* 5, no. 4 (October 2019): 34.

[4] Saint John Paul II, *Catechesi Tradendae*, Vatican.va, art. 55.

echesis in the past, Saint John Paul II insisted that any memorization in catechesis today ought to be "intelligent" and "original." That is, we ought to propose only the most important things to be remembered, and not a volume of content that cannot "at the same time be understood."[5] Additionally, our methods ought to be creative, interesting, and even fun. The *U.S. National Directory for Catechesis* adds that "learning by heart" should be done "gradually, flexibly, and never slavishly."[6] Only in this way will learners experience the delight of a close personal possession of the treasury given to us by God. Interestingly, Saint John Paul II also offers a list of what Catholics ought to hold in their memory, and the first three categories on his list are "the words of Jesus, of important Bible passages, of the Ten Commandments."[7] This kind of personal reverence for Scripture, not always integral to Catholic life outside of the liturgy, can be life-giving for individuals, families, and communities.

Gayle Somers of Phoenix, Arizona, helps us to see, from a conversation in her home with her granddaughters, how Scripture regularly read can become Scripture remembered, and how this can make all the difference in our times of informal family catechesis with those we love:

> An artist friend of mine created a beautiful icon of Eve and Mary. I sat with my two granddaughters (then aged five and three) at their little table one day to show it to them (they had met my artist friend). Eve is on one side, under the tree of the forbidden fruit, with a snake coiled around her leg, and Mary is on the other side, under the tree of the cross (only the wood

---

[5] Cf. ibid.
[6] USCCB, *National Directory for Catechesis* (Washington, DC: USCCB Publishing, 2005), 102.
[7] Saint John Paul II, *Catechesi Tradendae*, Vatican.va, art. 55.

shows). Eve looks very sad; Mary is quite pregnant and is reaching out to Eve. The icon is rich
in color and depth; it begs to be explained!

So, I sat with the girls and asked them to
look at it. First, I asked who the two women
were. They knew right away, because we read
the Bible to them regularly; they get a Bible story every night at bedtime. Then I asked them
what they liked best about the icon. They each
mentioned several things (the gold all around
the edges, the colors in Mother Mary's dress,
etc.), and I added my own. Then, I asked, "Why
do you think Eve looks so sad?" The answer
came quickly from Seraphina, the oldest (and
self-designated spokeschild): "Because she dis-
obeyed God and ate the fruit she shouldn't have.
She sinned, and so do we. When Adam and Eve
ate that apple, I think that tree died." I said, "Yes,
lots of things died, even Adam and Eve." She replied, "And so do we." Then: "Why do you think
Mother Mary is reaching out to Eve?" There
was a pause. I asked: "Who is in Mother Mary's
tummy?" Right away: "Jesus." Then, "What did
Jesus do for us on this tree over here?" Again,
"He died for us, for our sins." I asked, "What
happened to him after that?" "He rose from the
dead," with me adding, "And so do we, right?
We don't have to be afraid of death anymore,
do we?" Then I suggested, "So, perhaps Mary
is telling Eve not to be sad, because everything
that went wrong under this tree" (pointing to
the tree in the garden) "was put right with this
tree" (pointing to the cross). Seraphina said,

"Yes, Mary is telling her not to be sad. This painting should have written on it right here" (pointing to the bottom gold space), "'Do not be sad. Do not be sad.'"

This was a very rich moment for me. The girls were so young, but without much prompting, they completely understood all the imagery and its meaning because they knew the details of Eve's story and of Mother Mary's that they've heard over and over from their nightly Bible stories. I told Seraphina it was right to want to write, "Do not be sad" on the icon, because now we can all have hope, not sadness — surely a true "Gospel moment" with my grandchildren.

SERVING THE CONVERSION PROCESS

How we teach in this movement of explanation also must help facilitate Christian conversion. In catechesis, conversion becomes possible when what we come to deeply understand begins to change us. But how do we lead people into deeper understanding? A law of human nature comes into play here: Deep understanding is not happened upon passively.

Educational experts have for many years distinguished between "active" and "passive" learning. Active learning is thought to take place when participants take responsibility for what they are learning.[8] Only when we are actively engaged does what we are learning become important to us. From this position, we begin to think for ourselves and want to understand.

On the other hand, passive learning takes place when we are stuck in the mode of unthinking receptivity. I teach univer-

---

[8] Cf. Jennifer L. Faust and Donald R. Paulson, "Active Learning in the College Classroom," *Journal on Excellence in College Teaching* 9:2 (1998): 3–24.

sity students for a living. I know (from my own experience as a student as well!) that it is possible to sit in a class, take good notes, study those notes, take an exam, give the class material back on the exam, and in the end receive a very strong "A" — and yet throughout the whole process never actually think about what is being learned. Passive learning or unthinking receptivity might be effective for passing a class, but it is not at all helpful in becoming a disciple. Passive learning in catechesis results in a passive Christianity, which does not hold up amidst today's cultural challenges. Therefore, passivity is the great enemy of an evangelizing catechesis.

It must be our priority to help our students to think as they are being taught. Only with an alert engagement with what we teach can a deep understanding of the Faith and conversion of heart be a possible outcome.

Let's explore some ways to teach that encourage active learning.

Curiosity

In chapter 5, we explored the importance of provoking curiosity in our students. If we've sufficiently done this in our early stages, we will see the fruits of our labors here as we begin to teach. But, especially for those with short attention spans — which means just about everyone today — this work of stirring up interest must continue in this step.

Provocative teaching will help people to stay interested and engaged. Bob Sutton of Altoona, Pennsylvania, gives us one example of how he stirs up curiosity as he teaches:

> Every year I taught my twelfth graders, I began my lesson on the existence and nature of God by spending a full period watching a PBS documentary on ants without any explanation or

connection being provided. I simply told the students that the information in the documentary was important, and the documentary was interesting enough to hold their attention after that. Invariably I would see students leaving the classroom scratching their heads or asking me what it had to do with religion.

The next day, we discussed the content of the video and I asked basic questions that laid the groundwork for discussing God's existence. Is it plausible that the intricate and unbelievably organized structure of ant society truly happened by accident? All species of ant seem to function with a clear sort of "programming" toward specific ends. Do they actually have purpose, or is this simply some sort of genetic illusion? Discussion is encouraged on these points, so that the students' opinions and perspectives on the answers to these questions are all valued and developed in a class discussion format. This is so effective that I am then able to refer to the ants throughout the year, both in discussion and in notes, as a basis for discussing not only divine nature, but creation, human nature, and many other key doctrines as well.

Learning Capacities

In an evangelizing catechesis, their Catholic way of engaging reality is stretching and growing. But not every group — or every person in a group — learns the same. Adapting our methods to the learning capacities of those we teach, especially if they are children or adolescents, is essential.

Psychologist Joseph White shares this important observation: "Attention span is about equal to age in minutes, up to the early twenties (when the prefrontal cortex is fully grown). That means if we try to deliver a 10-minute talk to a group of second graders, almost every one of them will have tuned us out after 7 or 8 minutes!" As overwhelming as this might sound for us catechists, there is good news, too. White continues, "Science indicates that involving multiple senses in learning actually 're-sets' the attention clock. For example, if we are telling a story to a group of young learners and we introduce a new visual aid or have them move around, they will pay more attention to the material we are presenting."[9] Actively engaging young people in catechesis, therefore, is going to require methodological creativity. Of course, we can be tempted here to fall into the rut of constantly planning a never-ending stream of experiential activities that do not actually promote real thinking, let alone a deeper understanding of the content we are charged to communicate. Always, we've got to evaluate ourselves: Have I helped them to more deeply understand what God has entrusted to me to teach?

Questions

One way to promote real thinking, no matter the age group, is to ask frequent questions. Of course, knuckles will not be rapped with a ruler if an answer is incorrect. Instead, with patience and a smile, we can build a culture of friendly interaction and discussion. I had the privilege of watching master catechist Barbara Morgan in action in her RCIA process. For Barbara, good teaching meant entering into a lively conversation, where she would freely connect to the experience of people in the room and ask lots of questions. She taught systematically and presented the

---

[9] Joseph D. White, "Children's Catechesis: Five Ways Psychology Can Inform Catechesis," *The Catechetical Review* 3, no. 3 (July 2017): 33.

Faith in a comprehensive way, but it all happened conversationally, which kept participants interested and engaged.

Nicole Lancour of Williamsburg, Virginia, knows the importance of this dynamic for children's catechesis. She explains:

> As a Catechesis of the Good Shepherd catechist, I am trained to ask "wondering questions" when introducing children to Scripture. These questions are meant to guide the children toward their own moments of realization with Scripture. For example, when reading The Parable of the Lost Sheep (Luke 15), I ask, "Why do you think the sheep got lost?" and "How do you think the sheep felt when he was found?" While theologically, we know that this passage is about reconciliation, for the child it becomes a place of encounter with the Word, where the child can be moved by the Scriptures in a spiritual way.

While these kinds of "wondering questions" are helpful in engaging the imaginations of children, we are all created to be in wonder before the Mystery of God. Questions that evoke wonder will be important no matter the age of those we teach.

In catechizing adolescents or adults, what if we ask, "Does anyone have any questions?" and no one puts a hand up? In such a scenario, it is a mistake to presume that everyone gets it and continue on with more teaching. Instead, when this happens, I encourage my students to presume passivity, or worse, that no one is paying attention. Rather than continuing to teach, begin a focused conversation. And we shouldn't only ask questions with one-word answers (e.g., "What term do we use for the dogma of Mary being preserved from original sin?"); instead, be sure to include questions that require more from them (e.g., "How would you respond to this objection to Mary's perpetual virginity?"). Asking challenging questions always must be done with kindness, patience, and good humor — and helping them to articulate an accurate answer may take some time. But when a challenging question is posed and thoughtfully considered, real thinking can take place. This is frequently where authentic catechesis begins.

There are many other ways, of course, to promote active learning and deeper understanding in those we form. Teaching concretely — that is, with helpful analogies, examples, stories, and imagery (to name just a few ideas) — not only promotes understanding, but what we teach also will be more likely to be remembered. Brad Bursa of Cincinnati, Ohio, shares with us one example of teaching in a visually palpable way, imparting an idea that I'll bet his teenagers still remember:

> Many of today's teens are incredibly receptive, but passively so. Fostering interaction, especially in a lecture-based setting, can be a real struggle for youth who engage with reality experientially and visually. Recently, I was attempting to explain the call to holiness and the concept of Christian witness to teens. I explained that members of the early church were called "saints," not in that they were all canonized (or canonizable!), but that they were to be "reference points" for others — windows that allow the light of the Son to shine into the world. We happened to be in a chapel with stained-glass windows, so I invited everyone to leave their seats and to head outside in the midday heat. With everyone gathered, I asked them what they noticed about

the windows. They observed that they were jet black from the outside, that they did not allow one to see into the Church, and that the designs were unintelligible. Then, we went back inside and viewed the windows from a vantage point of being inside the church. It is an entirely different experience, at least during the day, as the light illuminates the whole image. I invited the youth to imagine themselves as a stained-glass image. Our lives are made up of many little pieces, which may often seem like disparate and broken parts. However, when we allow Christ to illuminate the whole of our lives — all of the fragments — suddenly the whole comes into view and it is beautiful to behold. However, we can only see the whole image from inside of the Church. Our lives become intelligible to us from within the communion of the Church and only when we allow the light of Christ to strike the whole of us. I taught that we are invited to allow the light of the Son to penetrate every part, every fragment of our lives, transforming our lives and making them wholly intelligible. From this position of being within the Church and allowing Christ's light to touch the whole of our lives, our very lives (every piece, every iconic symbol, every beveled edge) refer to the Source of the light.

Christ-Centered and Trinitarian

Finally, the content of our catechesis must be about the Father, the Son, and the Holy Spirit. It is the glad tidings of the Gospel of Christ that we must proclaim and teach. Just as the apostles preached Christ crucified in the early Church, sparking many to become disciples, so too, today the call to know and follow the Word Made Flesh and Splendor of the Father is the answer to each person's deepest desires. My mentor Barbara Morgan frequently suggested in her classes that catechists write at the top of every lesson plan: What does this have to do with Jesus and the love of the Trinity?

There is one last important point. As we can see, an evangelizing catechesis is not merely conceptual or informational. It is also not stuck in an endless monologue of sharing our own personal experiences. The evangelizing catechist, invested in helping passive participants become interested seekers, adopts a distinctive (and perhaps new) posture. While teaching, while explaining, the catechist also proposes. What is being proposed? Nothing less than the choice to become a disciple, to live one's life in Christ. Therefore, each of us must embrace an important new dynamic in our teaching: We must frequently employ the language of invitation. While teaching the content of the Faith, the catechist proposes life with God in Christ. This is the broader context through which every aspect of the Catholic Faith finally becomes intelligible. Our learners can't miss this about Catholicism, or they miss what is most essential. Returning frequently to this invitation to friendship with God, to loving communion, to the adventure of living in the light amidst growing darkness — this is fundamentally how the teaching of the content of Revelation becomes an experience of evangelization.

In these ways, then, the explanation step becomes an opportunity to learn the mind of Christ, to come to understand more deeply the way of discipleship — and, in the end, to receive the invitation to invest ourselves into communion with God within the Church.

It should be obvious that simply receiving this invitation

isn't enough. In the final two movements of catechesis (which we will discuss in the next two chapters), the entire dynamic will shift.

PUTTING "EXPLANATION" INTO PRACTICE

Let's take a few moments to identify ideas for this movement of explanation, using again our sample doctrine of angels. Look back through the section in the *Catechism* on angels (328–36). As you look through it again, circle or underline the sentences that seem to be key points about the doctrine, those you think would be most useful for your students. From all the points you underlined or circled, pick the three points that you think are most important for your students to understand, or that would best spark the students' interest. Be sure that at least one of these teaching points shows in what way the doctrine on angels is clearly rooted in the life and work of Christ. Keep in mind that, while there might not be only one correct set of teaching points, the outline of the *Catechism* often provides a clue about what the most important points may be. Curriculum guidelines will also be helpful.

Having identified what you will teach, you can now ask yourself how you will teach in ways that spark active learning. You might consider strategies for evoking curiosity as well as how to include creative analogies and stories. Write down a few questions by which you might help participants to more deeply seek. Finally, what can we learn from the angels about being in communion with God — and what opportunities might there be in this catechesis to invite students deeper into the Christian life?

CHAPTER EIGHT

Application-Discipleship
Growing Roots

A n important moment is upon us. The new plant must now extend its own roots further into the soil if it is to thrive. If our students are going to make the gift of faith their own, they must at some point form their own convictions and new commitments. Thus, the dynamic of catechesis changes in this step: We move now from the proclamation and explanation of the teaching of Christ to the cultivation of a response on the part of our students.

Saint John Paul II wrote that one of the greatest dangers facing the layperson in the contemporary world is the tendency to separate faith from life.[1] Within the process of catechesis, we must give our students opportunities to bring their life and their own personal convictions into unity with the Faith they profess. These must be integrated. Within a catechetical paradigm, application-discipleship is a critical movement in forming a person in the Christian life.

"Firm and well-thought-out convictions," writes Saint John Paul II, "lead to courageous and upright action."[2] However, there is one important caveat: New convictions do not automatically lead to a change in how we live. For most of us, we can easily become convicted of something we'd like to change in our life, and yet do nothing with that conviction. Catechetical explanation, therefore, is not enough. Something else is needed. Any passive engagement (mentioned in the last chapter) with the Faith must become something that is active, something that is willed, if a person is going to become a disciple through catechesis.

The first of these movements of an evangelizing catechesis, preparation, helped bring about a "calculated disengagement" from everyday life so that we could give our attention to what is proclaimed and explained. This application step can be best understood as a "calculated re-engagement." What we have received in catechesis must not only be understood, but it also must come to vivify our everyday life.

Two things are needed. Those we teach have to first apply the content of the Gospel (proclaimed and explained) to the concrete situations in which they think and live. They have to set their view of reality side by side with the Catholic worldview in order to see the points of convergence and of dissonance. Next, we catechists have to help learners to take steps forward. It is not enough to compare and contrast our own personal beliefs with

---

[1] John Paul II, *Christifideles Laici*, accessed April 20, 2020, Vatican.va, par. 2.
[2] John Paul II, *Catechesi Tradendae*, accessed April 20, 2020, Vatican.va, par. 22.

Catholic Faith and life. To be a disciple, we must take the plunge and begin to conform ourselves to the way of Christ.

It is perhaps unrealistic to imagine that all of this can happen in a short (fifteen- to thirty-minute) block of time. But when we set aside this time during each catechesis to apply the content, and also to give learners chances to take steps toward Christ, over time real transformation becomes possible.

APPLICATION: ITS TWO DIRECTIONS

Let's first consider how we might help our students apply the Faith. There are two primary ways.

1) Cultural Application

Each of us lives immersed in culture. There are various cultural milieus that influence how we think, feel, respond to life's stimuli, communicate, make decisions, and act.

Every family has its own culture. Our ethnic heritage influences us, as does the era into which we were born and the part of our country in which we live. Of course, when we consider something as ubiquitous as the entertainment industry, we can speak, too, of an influential popular culture. Each of these cultural influences (to name just a few) in a person's life is going to have points of consistency with the Gospel message, as well as points of inconsistency. The Second Vatican Council points out that these various cultures from which we come and in which we live contain elements and tendencies that are in need of being "healed, ennobled, and perfected" by the light of Christ.[3]

For the catechist, then, the important question related to culture is this: Considering the various cultures in which our learners live, in what ways do these cultures promote and elevate what we are teaching; and in what ways is the teaching of Christ

---

[3] Second Vatican Council, *Lumen Gentium,* accessed April 20, 2020, Vatican.va, par. 17.

challenged or even undermined by the cultural experiences of our students? These questions are so important because the believing disciple must learn to navigate her way through the complex influences of culture as a believing disciple. Culture also needs to be engaged and transformed by the one who follows Christ. This is for the sake of one's own growth in holiness, and it is precisely how the disciple evangelizes culture. He must heal, ennoble, and perfect the world in which he lives, as he himself is being healed, ennobled, and perfected by the grace of God. Monsignor Kelly explains: "Our mission is to bring the faith to today's real world. This means being sensitive to the modern world's concerns and also seeking to understand critically its thought patterns and language. It must be, however, our humble conviction that we have the values and truth that this modern world is actually seeking."[4]

What does this look like in practical terms? Those involved in marriage preparation can assist engaged couples to measure personal tendencies and communication habits that arise out of one's family of origin, for their consistency (or inconsistency) with the nature of Christlike love and sacramental marriage. As any married couple knows well, the collision of worldviews stemming from differing family backgrounds can make for challenging experiences, especially in the first years of marriage.

In a different scenario, learning the Theology of the Body ought to be accompanied by some application to popular culture. Young men and women need to gain the ability to critically evaluate the messages so aggressively conveyed in movies, music, and advertisements for whether they are speaking the truth about love. Furthermore, it is only when we begin to assess our cultural influences in the light of Christ that we will become

---

[4] Monsignor Francis D. Kelly, *The Mystery We Proclaim — Second Edition: Catechesis for the Third Millennium* (Huntington, IN: Our Sunday Visitor, 1997), 63.

active protagonists in helping establish what Saint John Paul II called a "civilization of truth and love."[5]

We should note that cultural application can remain entirely on the conceptual level. We can do this kind of thinking and discovery without having to make any adjustments in how we personally choose to think or live. While cultural application is necessary in the journey toward holiness and missionary discipleship, it is incomplete without a more personal incorporation of what has been received in catechesis.

2) Personal Application

How, then, does the content of the catechesis apply to us personally? When considering this, it is helpful not to repeatedly fixate on one or two dimensions of life (such as morality or how we pray), since every aspect of a person's life is meant to be transfigured in Christ. Rather, we need a broader paradigm that helps us consider the totality of a person's interior life and actions, as the whole person is called to the fullness of Christian life.

It may be helpful here to remember what the Church calls the "six tasks of catechesis."[6] Each of these is phrased in the 1997 *General Directory for Catechesis* in terms of some task that the catechist provides: knowledge of the faith, liturgical education, moral formation, teaching to pray, education for community life, and missionary initiation. But what if we instead envisioned them from the perspective of the catechized person, as dimensions of life in Christ that need development? Seen in this way, the possibilities for personal application are many:

1. Our knowledge of the Faith and the content of our personal beliefs and convictions

---

[5] John Paul II, *Evangelium Vitae*, accessed April 20, 2020, Vatican.va, par. 6.
[6] See *General Directory for Catechesis*, accessed April 20, 2020, Vatican.va, par. 85–86.

2. Our investment into the liturgy and our sacramental life
3. The process by which we discern and make moral choices
4. How we pray
5. How we live as disciples in relation to other people within our families and communities
6. Our response to our missionary vocation, whatever that might look like in the concrete circumstances of each person's life

Each of these "tasks" represents an important facet of living as a Catholic disciple of Christ.

OPPORTUNITIES TO GROW

Coming to see the cultural and personal application of the Faith is important. But, at some point in the process of catechesis, learners must be encouraged to choose to take steps forward. We can be certain that every such movement in the Christian life is a graced movement; that is, the grace of God has gone before our students and is enlightening and empowering them as they consider taking such steps. It is as the *Catechism* tells us: "Grace is favor, the free and undeserved help that God gives us to respond to his call" (1996). The catechist, then, strives to cooperate with the movement of grace in all the details of teaching life in Christ; of proposing life in Christ; and finally, in inviting those entrusted to us to take steps into this life.

Of course, as our learners probe the content of Christianity and come to understand what their "yes" means, responses will vary. To the degree that an individual responds positively, he or she will need personal encouragement and guidance in taking steps forward. Consider the example of Saint Andrew the apostle. As he took his first steps, following after Jesus upon first hearing him teach, the Lord invited him on to "come, and you will see" (Jn 1:39). We can be confident that Our Lord will say the same to our learners as they are inspired to earnestly seek him.

Not everyone will respond as we hope. The catechist (and this is even more true for parents) must continue to pour out love and respect, especially when those we are forming do not take the steps forward that we hope they will. This is the Christlike, self-giving love to which we are called, for Our Lord did not coerce, but instead respected the freedom of those in whom he invested so deeply.

What, then, might this movement of personal discipleship look like, practically speaking? Let's examine a few examples.

Part of growing in confidence in the life of prayer is gaining strategies to overcome distractions. When I was a parish youth minister, I asked our parish deacon to speak to our confirmation candidates about prayer. As he walked into the room, he asked, "James, do you trust me?" After all the red flags and ringing mental alarms receded (don't such questions always elicit such a response?), I responded with an enthusiastic "yes," because I knew him well and trusted him. He looked me in the eye and said, "Then just roll with what we're going to do." He offered an insightful thirty-minute introduction to prayer. He then smiled, surveyed the group, and said, "Okay, everybody, get up and follow me," and he walked out the door. There were more than a hundred catechists and teenagers in the room, and we all looked at each other, got up, and followed the deacon. He walked toward the perpetual adoration chapel, and I thought, "What a great idea! He's introduced us to prayer, and now he's going to give us a chance to practice what he's taught us." But he walked right past the chapel. The next building to be approached and then passed was the church. And now I really was getting nervous, because there was nothing else out there. He took us out into the parking lot, not far from a busy intersection with lots of typical busy-intersection sounds. He gathered us around him and said, "Now I want to teach you how to pray amidst distraction. Our prayer on this property is very important, but Christians also must know how to pray in the world." After giving us some specific tips for moving beyond distractions, he then invited us to pray two decades of the Rosary with him, giving us a chance to try the skills he had just taught us.

In this example, we might remember from chapter 4 the apprenticeship paradigm. This deacon taught and showed, but also gave us a chance to try these skills for ourselves, in the hope that they might grow into something we could do on our own.

An evangelizing catechesis encourages strides forward, whether these steps are confident or shaky. In this movement of application and discipleship, there will always be a note of gentle encouragement and challenge in the catechist's words. And with these invitations, we will sometimes see those we're forming take steps in simple, yet profound ways. Jake Stanley recounts two experiences of young people responding to God's promptings, even without Jake being directly involved:

> A few months ago, our high school ministry took a weeklong mission trip to Gallup, New Mexico, a very poor diocese in the United States. While there, we served those in need alongside the members of several religious orders, including the Missionaries of Charity and the Little Sisters of the Poor. A month or so after the trip, I bumped into one of the teens who attended and asked how the rest of her summer had been. She went on to tell me that

she and several of her friends had been getting together on their own to go to a local soup kitchen to prepare and serve food there. I was amazed that these teens had done this without any organization from myself or other parish volunteers. They heard the invitation to serve and responded generously.

A different time, Jake was surprised to see this instance of young people taking steps forward into the Christian life on their own:

One Saturday morning, I was at our parish, gathering some supplies. As I arrived, daily Mass was finishing. I looked up to see a crowd of our high school teens pouring out of the church doors into the parking lot. They were laughing and talking to each other. There was such an infectious joy in their community. I went up to talk with them to find out what was going on that they were all at daily Mass, unprompted by myself or other staff. They had all simply decided that they wanted to come to Mass together on a Saturday morning and go out to breakfast afterwards.

In our ministry, we often challenge teens to expand their prayer life through daily Mass, Eucharistic Adoration, and personal prayer. Sometimes, it seems that the advice falls on deaf ears. This experience reminded me how important it is to continually invite them. When young people freely choose to live this out, it becomes possible and even attractive for other teens.

Sister Athanasius Munroe, OP, of Ann Arbor, Michigan, shows us with wonderful detail how she helps her nine-year-old students in her Catholic school learn about the call to evangelize. She also provides them an opportunity to take a step forward in planting the seeds of the Gospel in another person's heart.

I had been teaching the children that each one of us is responsible for proclaiming Jesus to others. If we loved Jesus, we would want others to love him, too. Each student selected someone they knew who they thought did not know Jesus: who didn't live his teachings or go to church. In front of them, I planted some seeds, explaining that each of us is called by Jesus to sow the seeds of his word in the hearts of others. But once we sow, we must "water" the seeds through constant prayer, and then wait to see if it sprouts; it is up to God to give the growth. Each student wrote his person's name on a sticky note and kept it on his desk to remind him to pray for that person.

From there, I taught them the basic message of the Gospel found in the Acts of the Apostles. I then announced the project: We would be making a video to share this good news with others. I gave each student a set of questions to help them prepare their segment, directed them to the right place to find ideas to jump-start their answers, and then turned them loose. They worked incredibly hard, and even took them home as homework. Finally, we prayed (a lot!), asking the Holy Spirit for a loan on the graces of confirmation, to allow the students to be convicting witnesses to Jesus.

And the Holy Spirit totally blew me away. The things the students heard in class echoed in their heart and came back to me, transformed in a way that showed exactly how much they had made it their own. (And that is exactly why it is so important to create the space in your lesson plan for them to take it in. That is where they make it their own.)

"God's love can't be beat, by your mom or dad. ... He loves you to the moon and back, infinite times! ... He made you to love him."

This was pouring out of little "Matthew's" heart. I was astounded. Matthew's mother and I had been talking throughout the year about ways to help him stay grounded in the Faith. Shortly after they married, Matthew's father had left her. Since then, he had been going through spouses faster than the Samaritan woman. Formerly, her son idolized his dad. This year, he had begun to realize that not everything in Dad's life was consistent with what Matthew was being taught. It was reaching that point of crisis.

Matthew had made his choice. He poured out everything he was learning about the Father's love, in hopes of reaching his dad. And he began to pray for his conversion.

ABILITIES NEEDED BY THE DISCIPLE

Stories like these raise the question: What are the habits of a disciple? It's a harmless enough question, unless we ask it a bit more pointedly: By the time a young person graduates from high school (or the neophyte year of the RCIA process), what are the habits and disciplines she needs to be growing into in order to live a vibrant adult Catholic life? Asked like this, such a question becomes quite challenging for us catechists.

Certainly, these habits, skills, and abilities are going to be best learned within the family, which Saint John Paul II called the "school of following Christ."[7] Yet, many parents today are not taking up the Christian formation of their children in a meaningful way. In these cases, we have to ask where these habits and abilities of a disciple will be learned. The importance of the catechist and the time of catechesis increase exponentially, especially in these situations. We must do everything we can to support our families and help them become what they are, as Saint John Paul II once wrote.[8] Additionally, we must consider how our time of catechesis can help equip those we teach with the disciplines and skills a missionary disciple will need in the twenty-first century.

Over the course of the years we hopefully have with them, we can help our students develop a disciple's habits through this movement of application-discipleship. We can help them grow in their ability to read Scripture daily, pray from the heart, actively and intelligently participate in the sacramental life, pray the liturgy of the hours, offer praise and worship to God, and develop a heart for those in need and a consistent practice of reaching out to them. We can also help them give confident testimony to the goodness of God, to "give an explanation to anyone who asks you for a reason for your hope" (1 Pt 3:15), and to answer difficult questions about the Faith. As is the case for all of us, they will need to become more capable of

---

[7] John Paul II, *Familiaris Consortio*, accessed April 20, 2020, Vatican.va, par. 39.
[8] Cf. ibid., art. 17.

inviting others to know the One who created us for the eternal life and love that we have begun to experience.

Some might wonder how we can do this kind of discipleship training in the short time we have with them in catechesis. While this application-discipleship time is a good place for it, opportunities abound to form them more practically. We've already discussed the idea of using our prayer time more strategically to form them in the habits of prayer. When we spend time pondering Scripture with them, this is a chance to have them also open up their Bibles to find the passage, stirring in them an interest to spend time in the text themselves. Drawing upon the actual words, signs, symbols, and gestures present in our sacramental rites puts them into contact with the incarnational language of the rites, which will help them to move "from the visible to the invisible, from the sign to the thing signified, from the 'sacraments' to the 'mysteries'" (CCC 1075) when they are present and invested in the celebration of a sacrament. When we understand catechesis to be not just an explanation, but also the place to form disciples, we will search for opportunities to help them form the habits and dispositions they need.

Whether we help them to apply the content of the lesson or to take concrete steps forward as disciples, many are the ways this step can be carried out. We might set aside time for small discipleship groups so that a more personal and engaging conversation can take place. Or, we might give them time to reflect and pray and come to their own personal resolutions. We could watch a film clip and offer a chance to critically engage it in the larger group. Or we might offer people a chance to ask the thoughtful questions that arise out of the explanation step.

However we choose to allow opportunities for application and discipleship, this time is critically important. It is not a time for the catechist to apply and make connections for participants, but rather a chance for the students to make these discoveries themselves. Engaging their freedom in this way is a necessary step in the discipleship process. Their living of the Christian life depends upon this life progressively becoming their own. Allowing for application and response provides the real possibility for this to take place. As Jean Mouroux puts it, "Only those free acts which incarnate faith can cause faith to take deep root in the soul, can personalize faith, and insert it into life as a saving influence."[9]

PUTTING "APPLICATION-DISCIPLESHIP" INTO PRACTICE

We'll begin first with application before we move to discipleship. Let's first consider the cultural aspects impacting learners: the influence of friends, political ideas, movies, social media and other internet sites, family situations, etc. Thinking again about our sample topic of angels, *what is one way* in which the surrounding cultures respect and promote the existence of angels? And what is *one way* in which our cultural influences undermine the truth about angels in the lives of those being catechized?

We can also consider means of personal application — though both need not be done every time. It can be helpful to first think about the personal application to our lives as catechists, in order to help others see that application in their own lives. Thus, we can answer this question ourselves: What about this doctrine of the angels do I find utterly amazing, and what aspects would I most like to share with others?

Then, we can answer the following questions about those being catechized:

---

[9] Jean Mouroux, *From Baptism to the Act of Faith*, trans. Sister M. Elizabeth, IHM, and Sister M. Johnice, IHM (Boston: Allyn and Bacon Inc., 1964), 25.

- Why does it really matter to this person's life that angels are real?
- What would be lost for this person if he or she never knew this to be true?

The answers to these questions can then help us think of what we could discuss in this personal *application* time. For now, we can answer these questions as they relate to our sample topic of angels, but then consider using these questions for preparing to teach other themes as well.

Finally, how can we help them take steps forward as disciples? Perhaps we could provide participants with a number of scriptural passages to look up that feature the angels and encourage them to set time aside to learn and pray with these passages. We might also want to introduce them to the words of Saint Basil, who wrote: "Beside each believer stands an angel as protector and shepherd leading him to life."[10] Each of us has our own guardian angel — eye-opening news! Encouraging them to acknowledge the depths of God's personal care, and also to begin asking their angels to pray for them and protect them and lead them to eternity, is a beautiful step forward into the life of being a disciple.

---

[10] Saint Basil, *Adv. Eunomium III*, 1: PG 29, 656B, quoted in CCC 336.

CHAPTER NINE

Celebration

Blossoms and the Promise of Fruitfulness

In the previous chapter, we explored a fourth movement in an evangelizing catechesis, one that allows space for application and for a personal response on the part of those we teach. As we consider our ultimate aspirations for our students, what is the highest, most sanctifying response that we hope for in them as they move toward discipleship? What response does the saint make to God?

Monsignor Kelly points us to an important mark of how the person who truly sees the Christian life for what it is responds to the proclamation of the Christian message. He writes, "If the catechetical process begins in prayerful attentiveness and openness to the Word of God ..." (we can remember here those initial movements in the preparation step):

> ... I believe that it must also end in prayerful gratitude and praise to God. This attitude of thanksgiving and praise is paradigmatic for all of Christian life. We look at the "wonderful things" God has done in the Creation and Redemption and are spontaneously impelled to prayer and praise. This must be a major part and the climax of a catechetical process and methodology that is deeply rooted in the Church's own faith and self-understanding.[1]

In other words, in catechesis we not only receive and study the word of God, we also learn how to respond to it as disciples of Christ.

There are, of course, many ways we can respond to God. There are times of deep understanding and delight. There are times of difficulty and questioning. Each of us goes through different seasons, to be sure. But the very highest response of the disciple — the response that best expresses what arises in the person who knows deeply that the whole of reality has been created from love and is invited into a self-giving love that is eternal — is the response of gratitude and praise. As we grow in holiness and are more and more conformed to Christ, we will see with increasing clarity the providential, loving plan of God and his divine grace mysteriously at work in the world. Indeed, this vision of true reality forms the context, the backdrop, of life in Christ — even as we work through questions, difficulties, and experience times of desolation and suffering. The one who

---

[1] Francis D. Kelly, *The Mystery We Proclaim*, 146–47.

grows in sanctity comes to see everything as gift. And in the end, our gratitude will become "eternalized" when we, cooperating with the saving grace of God, join the saints and angels in their forever praise of the Father, the Son, and the Holy Spirit. Learning and living in the Church's gratitude for all that God has done opens us to the life enjoyed by the communion of saints. When the whole Church in heaven and on earth celebrates the Eucharist (based on a Greek word, *eucharistein*, which means "to give thanks"), we can recall here the upward movements of adoration, praise, and thanksgiving. These form the content of what the disciple offers to God, united to the Blessed Trinity with all the saints and angels forever. And we saints-in-the-making must grow into these same dispositions so that they become our own.

Just as catechesis teaches us how to respond to the gift of God's word through this fifth movement of celebration, so too does the Sacred Liturgy. There are two verbal expressions that sum up the response of the Church, the praying Mystical Body of Christ, to the liturgical proclamation of God's word: "Thanks be to God!" and "Praise to you, Lord Jesus Christ!" These responses, made day in and day out in our liturgical prayer, help us to verbalize gratitude and praise; and, if we are interiorly alert, they also stir up within us these same dispositions. In the liturgy, we are immersed in a culture of thanksgiving, adoration, self-giving love, and praise of God. Indeed, the reality of such a culture — animated by the exchange of love that is its center and heart — is why we refer to the liturgy as a "celebration." Timothy O'Malley puts it well: "The liturgy is a celebration not because it's always happy, always full of what we consider good news like winning the lottery or a national championship. It is a celebration because it is a public space where the world can partake in the festive news that love unto the end, divine love, is the meaning of the world."[2]

Perhaps we can see more clearly how the final movement of catechesis ought to be focused toward the same dynamic response we see modeled for us when the word is proclaimed in the liturgy. In catechesis, too, we must be led to these same dispositions: "Thanks be to God!" and "Praise to you, Lord Jesus Christ!"

After carefully cultivating the soil, planting and tending the seedling, watering and continual weeding — here in this position of gratitude is where the first blossoms of faith, communion, and charity begin to emerge. And we know that, with the appearance of these blossoms, fruit is soon to follow.

THE LAST FIVE MINUTES

The last minutes of a catechesis, therefore, are important. This is our final opportunity to help our learners be formed in positive dispositions that will stay with them, especially those of gratitude and praise.

Very frequently, the last five to ten minutes of a catechesis end up unplanned, a catchall time to tie up loose ends. Perhaps we didn't make as much progress as we had hoped through our lesson plan, and so we use this time to catch up. Or maybe we've zipped along at a much quicker pace through the catechesis, and it becomes a free time for more discussion, or to play a game, or to do whatever seems best.

Other possibilities also could present themselves. We might instinctively conclude our catechesis with a time of personal application or gentle challenge, before a quick closing prayer. We might organize small-group discussion. Or we might take the time to encourage them to take seriously the command to see Christ in the person in need.

---

[2] Timothy P. O'Malley, *Divine Blessing* (Collegeville, MN: Liturgical Press, 2019), 20.

It is important to set time aside in the previous movement of application for initiatives such as these. They are significant opportunities to grow as disciples. However, instead of taking up one of these approaches in our closing minutes, let's consider what it might look like to invite our students to experience (and even express!) gratitude to God for what they have received in this time of catechesis.

Of course, no human being can be forced to be grateful, let alone to offer praise. Rather, these are responses that arise from a person's heart. At most, the catechist can create an atmosphere that is conducive to the offering of gratitude to God.

Physical Environment

Just as the physical arrangement of the room is important in the preparation step, so too here at the end. Some simple transition may help learners to step out of application and into celebration, ready for something new.

So, maybe we turn down lights and light a candle. Or, we could invite children to depart their desks and gather around a prayer space, allowing an opportunity for a few intimate words of encouragement and an invitation to pray. Perhaps we could leave the classroom and quietly walk to the chapel or the church. Larann Wilson of Oklahoma City, Oklahoma, describes a particular instance when she did this to introduce the children to the beauty of reverence for God:

> I was teaching the middle school class about the burning bush, the presence of God, and sacredness. We remained in the church as we read through the passage in Exodus. Nearing the end of the session, I asked them to remove their shoes as I had, and we quietly walked into the Eucharistic chapel. I modeled qui-

et reverence, and they followed my gestures. We sat together in front, and I talked to them about this holy ground and how Christ is present in the Eucharist. They asked many questions about the chapel and the Eucharist. To end our time together, I led them in a guided meditation prayer. They enjoyed it so much, they asked the following week to return to the chapel! Above all, I was moved by the one child who remained in the chapel praying for an extra five minutes after us. You could sense his gratitude for the time in Our Lord's presence because he had a much calmer spirit when he joined us.

While Larann is no advocate for shoeless adoration chapels, having the children remove their shoes in this instance, after prayerfully reading how Moses prepared himself to stand before the burning bush, provided a powerful connection between the Old Testament and the Eucharistic presence of Our Lord. And the simple change of environment signaled a new movement in gratitude toward the Lord.

Reconnecting to Jesus

These last five to ten minutes are not an opportunity to teach more content, but rather to take a step back and see the content of what they have learned in the light of love. We might recall here the helpful encouragement of the *Catechism*, that we make the love of the Lord accessible (cf. 25) no matter what it is we're teaching. Here is another important opportunity to make clear connections to the love of God.

For Saint Francis of Assisi, the love of God is most brightly seen in "the crib, the cross, and the Eucharist." Saint Francis's paradigm can be helpful for us catechists, as they are three particularly vivid connection points to the Revelation of Love's great Mystery. How can we relate the content of our lesson with the incarnational love of God; that is, the glorious fact that the invisible God assumed human nature and was born in Bethlehem to our great good? Or, how does understanding come in the light of the self-emptying love of Christ on the Cross? What about the supreme manifestation of Christ's love to us in this world, given as it is in his Body and Blood in the Holy Eucharist? Of course, everything contained in the life of Christ — indeed, everything in the entirety of the Bible — comes from love. But these three instances are extraordinary epiphanies and are helpful connection-points for the catechist who seeks to make the love of God accessible in the teaching of Christian doctrine.

Recentering ourselves in the love of God is always important, especially in the final moments of catechesis. Is there any better way to stir up gratitude and praise?

Beauty and Goodness

The Truth of Christ is both good and beautiful. The celebration step is a perfect place to help us to see this goodness and beauty, to bring it more clearly into focus so that it might strike the heart. It may be helpful here to impress once more upon participants that what we've received from God is good news. But rather than just being told that what we've studied is good and beautiful, is there a way that we can show them; or better, help them discover it for themselves?

This movement of celebration is a wonderful place for testimony. Perhaps we can tell them a story that helps them to see the goodness and beauty of what we've just learned. The catechist herself might have a story of the joy of intimate closeness with the Holy Spirit she experienced upon being confirmed, or a consolation received by persevering in prayer. Testimonies need not only be from the catechist — are there others in the classroom or the parish who might be able to offer such a testimony? Of course, here is a beautiful opportunity to share with them stories from the lives of the saints, stories that demonstrate the goodness of God and of our life in him as Christians.

These final moments of our catechesis are a perfect time to bring our participants into contact with the beauty so vividly expressed through certain works of art, music, literature, and film. An excerpt from the film *Life Is Beautiful* might help us to see what it looks like for a father and mother to pour out everything in love for their son. Reading a segment from *The Lord of the Rings* depicting the strengthening power of the waybread of the elves can help us see anew the miraculous capacity to sustain that our own "waybread," the Holy Eucharist, possesses. Listening to a hauntingly beautiful rendition of Mozart's *Ave Verum Corpus* while gazing upon Rembrandt's luminous painting of the body of Jesus being taken down from the cross (*The Descent from the Cross*) can give us the time to truly take in what God has done for us in Christ Jesus.

When it comes to utilizing sacred art in the catechetical setting, author and Catholic University of America catechetics professor Jem Sullivan proposes a slow, meditative approach like that of lectio divina rather than the typically quick consumerist approach frequently seen when we move briskly from painting to painting in an art museum or flip through pictures online. Sullivan points out that a meditative approach helps students "to acquire a new and deeper capacity for childlike wonder, to see with the 'eyes of faith' and hear with the 'ears of the heart.'"[3]

If we are able to conclude with time spent seeing the goodness and beauty of the truth we teach, it is possible that partic-

---

[3] Jem Sullivan, *The Beauty of Faith: Using Christian Art to Spread the Good News* (Huntington, IN: Our Sunday Visitor, 2009), 33.

ipants will leave catechesis with a disposition of peace and joy, in deeper wonder before the God who they know loves them.

EXPRESSING GRATITUDE AND PRAISE

The objective of both of these final two movements of application and celebration is for participants to respond to what they have received. And so, in this instance, we work to help them see the love of God as well as the goodness and the beauty of the Faith so that a desire to express gratitude and praise wells up in the hearts and minds of our students.

What does this response of gratitude and praise look like? So frequently, we can take inspiration from little ones. Sister Marie Celine Laird, OP, of Nashville, Tennessee, can tell us what it is like when three-year-olds are filled with gratitude and wonder toward God in the catechetical setting. She provides us these examples:

> This week as I was presenting the lesson on the Cenacle / Last Supper, one of the children pointed to the poster of the shepherd with the sheep. I asked them, "Who is the shepherd?" Most of the children replied, "Jesus." Then, I asked them a question I had asked them each time we did the Good Shepherd presentation: "Who are the sheep?" This was the first time a child answered, "We are!" Then, there was joy in the faces and bodies of the children. A couple of the children even jumped up and down. This is the good news of the Gospel. I've been waiting for the children to discover this truth — that they are the sheep. It is a profoundly joyful truth that touches their core because they know that if they are the sheep, then the shepherd loves them deeply.

Sister Marie Celine also relates this beautiful story: "One child's grandmother thanked me for teaching her son about Jesus. She relayed that 'Thomas' told her one day, 'Grammy, did you know that Jesus lives in my heart? Jesus lives in my heart!'" Whether we are three or seventy-three years old, it is when we come to these extraordinary discoveries ourselves that we experience the joy and delight of the Christian life. And when we are in such a position where we can clearly perceive the goodness and beauty of what he has given us, gratitude and praise are the only responses that do justice to our experience. Indeed, this is the very best ending point for our catechesis.

Perhaps some of us might be thinking, "Well, children are naturally inclined toward wonder and gratitude. But, I teach teenagers ..." Of course, it can take time for gratitude to grow in a person's heart, especially for those who are growing into adolescence and adulthood. We shouldn't be discouraged if indifference is all that is visible in the eyes that look back at us. Even if the apathy we see is an accurate representation of what is going on interiorly (and it isn't always a trustworthy indicator), thanksgiving, joy, and a desire to worship are dispositions that are learned over time by observing living witnesses and encountering Christ ourselves in word and sacrament. Grace Bellon of Charleston, South Carolina, a high school teacher, describes a creative assignment that gives her students an opportunity to take small steps toward expressing gratitude and praise to God:

> I have a reoccurring assignment at the end of each unit. Upon finishing the test, students have to "tweet" as a Bible character of their choosing from the stories we just covered. My students love this assignment. Diving deep into the mindset of what experiences might have been like for these people, they mix empathy,

humor, and events from modern culture. This not only helps them enter into Scripture better, it leaves them with smiles on their faces. Even students who may be apprehensive about test performance leave my classroom that day excited to complete their homework. That same evening, I collect my favorites and drop them into a simple PowerPoint presentation. At the beginning of class the next day, students vote on their favorite ones. Winners receive one bonus point, which I add to their test grade. While only some tweets and verbal exchanges result in obvious praise of God, the entire process is celebratory in nature, leaving everyone with good thoughts and happy feelings toward God and His word.

Two of Grace's personal favorites:

@Abram: We're soarin', flyn', there's not a star in heaven that won't be my descendant! #youknowyouwanttosing

("Look up at the sky and count the stars, if you can. Just so, he added, will your descendants be." Genesis 15:5)

@SamaritanWoman5Guyz: I thought it was jarring that Jesus even spoke to me ...

("'How can you, a Jew, ask me, a Samaritan woman, for a drink?'" John 4:9)

The very best way to express gratitude and praise to God is to do so in the direct encounter of prayer. Considering our objective in this movement of celebration, it's not difficult to imagine the kind of prayer that is best in most everyday catechetical circumstances. While there may be times where we choose to pray prayers of petition, or end in a meditative act of contrition, there is great benefit to concluding our catechesis offering thanks and praise to our loving God. As this becomes our characteristic way of concluding our study of God's word, we become more and more at home in gratitude and in loving God.

When a person chooses for himself to express real gratitude to God, it can be a pivotal step toward something very new. Consider the impact of being formed in the Christian life in a way that consistently accents the beauty and goodness of the truth. What if our religion departments and parish catechetical teams made a commitment that catechists would regularly end in this posture of gratitude and praise? Imagine the spiritual life of a child, teenager, or adult whose catechesis characteristically ends in a position of gratitude to God. When we live in thankfulness and receptivity, great things become possible.

PUTTING "CELEBRATION" INTO PRACTICE

Concluding our work on the angels, consider these important questions:

1. How is the existence of the angels "good news"? How is the fact of their existence, but also their loving adoration of God and their protective care for us, a truth that is both good and beautiful? What are some specific ways that we can help our learners see this goodness and beauty?

2. How will we encourage our students to respond to the moment of grace they have had in learning about the angels? How will we encourage them to

      let the truths just shared enter into their hearts rather than just being facts that they know?

3. How can our time of prayer encourage real expressions of gratitude and praise?

These questions provide a starting point for this movement of celebration — and may be helpful for many other topics you might find yourself teaching.

Epilogue

How does a catechist become a saint who contributes to the making of saints?

As we have considered in these pages, we must learn to live in and from communion with Jesus and teach in and from that same communion.

We must spend time with Our Lord, frequently encountering him especially in prayer and in the sacraments. When we invest ourselves into his work within us, the grace of God changes us, and we become fully alive. And so will our catechesis.

This continuing encounter with Jesus is the most important catalyst for our teaching. The catechist is very much like the Samaritan woman at the well. Her life-changing encounter with Jesus at the well propelled her through the streets of her whole town. We can imagine she went down every street! The words must have burst from her, with sheer joy and amazement: "Come see a man who told me everything I have done. Could he possibly be the Messiah?" (Jn 4:29).

Whether we are forming our own children or serving others in a parish or school, why is our own ongoing encounter with God so vital to our mission as catechists? Because fruitfulness in this work is only possible as we abide in the Vine who is Christ. We can imagine Our Lord smiling, as he himself answers this question for us: "Without me you can do nothing" (Jn 15:5).

Every catechist wants to be fruitful. We want our students to have a deeper desire for God and to live the life of a disciple. This is why we're in this — and it is why God has called us to this important work. The five movements considered in the second part of this book are each necessary to an evangelizing catechesis. This is because they are integral to the movement of Christian conversion itself. Our students will need time when they are free of distractions and genuinely open to the truth, beauty, and goodness of the Christian message (preparation). They will need to perceive the content of the Faith as a bold and loving announcement of life-altering Good News (proclamation). They will need to be actively engaged by a teaching that provokes their interest and desire to understand (explanation). What they learn must then be applied to their cultural surroundings and to their own life as a disciple, in a manner that invites them to take steps forward toward Jesus (application-discipleship). Finally, they will need to grow into the disposition of gratitude and in their desire to express this gratitude and praise to God, as these are fundamental dispositions in the child of God who knows the love of the Father.

As we come to understand these five movements and work toward incorporating them into our own methods of teaching, we can surely rely on the power and presence of the Holy Spirit, who wants to see our catechesis be fruitful even more than we do. As our students genuinely — and personally — encounter the transformative teaching of Christ, and as they take up the opportunities we've created for them to respond, real conversion becomes possible. Catechesis then takes its rightful position as a means of evangelization that cannot be set aside in the formation of Christians.

An evangelizing catechesis is, in fact, indispensable to the renewal of Catholic life in our parishes and schools. It is our way forward if those we form are to become a sanctifying and prophetic influence in the world, which is so full of desperate need. When we offer them such a catechesis, our students will discover the perennial invitation of the Father, the Son, and the Holy Spirit to enter into the life of divine love. Perhaps the great Saint Catherine of Siena put this invitation best: "Be who God meant you to be, and you will set the world on fire." By the grace of God and their own experience of being evangelized as they are catechized, those we teach will receive what they need to generously respond to this invitation.

Acknowledgments

I am grateful to so many good and generous people for the publication of this book.

The framework for many of the ideas contained in these pages originated in the classroom of Professor Barbara Morgan, whose passion for catechetics and catechetical methodology has made a lasting impression on many. I believe history will show that the investment Barbara and her husband, Gary, made in the Church's catechetical ministry — especially as Barbara founded the catechetics program at Franciscan University in 1994 — significantly advanced the renewal of catechesis in the United States and internationally. Barbara died last year, and many of us have keenly felt this loss. But it brings me joy that this holy woman met her Lord and Savior with eager anticipation, having lived a life of great fruitfulness for the kingdom.

I was so happy to work with Mary Beth Baker, whose tremendous insights as this book's editor were appreciated each step of the way.

There are a number of exceptional contributors to this book, beginning with my faculty colleague Dr. Scott Hahn. Scott's infectious love for the Triune God and for the Church has inspired countless tens of thousands of us across his career as professor, author, and speaker. I am humbled and deeply grateful that he accepted the invitation to write this book's foreword.

I would also like to thank those who contributed their own wisdom through the frequent testimonies found in each chapter. I especially wish to thank my longtime friend Jason Evert for his two compelling stories. Testimony is an irreplaceable element in an evangelizing catechesis — and is irreplaceable, too, in books describing an evangelizing catechesis!

I am grateful also to Teresa Hawes, Amy Roberts, Deacon Stephen Miletic, Elizabeth Siegel, Carole Brown, and Petroc Willey for their wisdom and assistance with parts of the book. Bill Keimig and the staff at the Catechetical Institute of Franciscan University very generously allowed me to adapt the practical application segments at the end of chapters 5 through 9 from exercises developed for the "ecclesial method" workshop available through the institute. Thank you, Bill!

Most of all, I want to express my deepest gratitude to my wife, Katrina, the first editor and chief encourager of this book. Thank you for your many sacrifices — so kindly and generously offered — that made it possible for me to write. Your intuitive contributions to the text throughout the writing process vastly improved every chapter. With you, and with our daughters Grace, Mairen, and Monica, I offer what is contained in these pages to our Heavenly Father in the hopes that (in some small way) it advances his kingdom and shows forth his glory.

Works Cited

Barron, Robert. *And Now I See: A Theology of Transformation*. New York: Crossroad Publishing Co., 1998.

———. *Heaven in Stone and Glass: Experiencing the Spirituality of the Great Cathedrals*. New York: Crossroad Publishing Co., 2002.

Bartkus, Justin. "The Home: A Catholic Subculture That Makes a Difference." *The Catechetical Review* 3, no. 2 (April 2017): 9–11.

Beckman, Jim. "Rethinking Youth Ministry." In *Becoming a Parish of Intentional Disciples*, edited by Sherry Weddell, 117–37. Huntington, IN: Our Sunday Visitor Inc., 2015.

Benedict XVI. "Homily for Eighth Centenary of the Birth of Pope Celestine V." July 4, 2010. In *The Power of Silence: Against the Dictatorship of Noise*, by Robert Cardinal Sarah with Nicolas Diat. Translated by Michael J. Miller. San Francisco: Ignatius Press, 2017.

———. *Sacramentum Caritatis*. Vatican Translation. Boston: Pauline Books and Media, 2007.

Blanchet, Alison. "Modern Man Listens More to Witnesses than to Tweeters." *The Catechetical Review* 5, no. 2 (April 2019): 38–39.

Catechism of the Catholic Church. 2nd ed. Washington, DC: Libreria Editrice Vaticana — United States Conference of Catholic Bishops, 2000.

Cavalletti, Sofia. *The Religious Potential of the Child: Experiencing Scripture and Liturgy with Young Children*. 2nd ed. Translated by Patricia M. Coulter and Julie M. Coulter. Chicago: Catechesis of the Good Shepherd Publications, 1992.

Chautard, Jean-Baptiste, OCSO *The Soul of the Apostolate*. Charlotte, NC: TAN Books, 1946.

Coleridge, Henry James. *The Life and Letters of Saint Francis Xavier*. Vol 1. London: Burns and Oates, 1872. https://archive.org/details/LifeLetters OfStFrancisXavierV1/page/n187. Accessed November 11, 2019.

Congregation for the Clergy. *General Directory for Catechesis*. Washington, DC: United States Conference of Catholic Bishops, 1997.

Corbon, Jean. *The Wellspring of Worship*. Translated by Matthew J. O'Connell. Mahwah, NJ: Paulist Press, 1988.

Davies, Bishop Mark. "St. John Vianney — A Saint of the New Evangelization, Part 3: The Holiness of the Catechist." *The Catechetical Review* 4, no. 1 (January 2018): 25–27.

Defos du Rau, Sister Hyacinthe, OP. "Come Follow Me: A New Model for Children's Catechesis." In *Liturgical Catechesis in the 21st Century: A School of Discipleship*, by James C. Pauley, 145–64. Chicago: Liturgy Training Publications, 2017.

Devananda, Angelo, ed. *Total Surrender: Mother Teresa*. Ann Arbor, MI: Servant, 1990.

Driscoll, Jeremy, OSB. *What Happens at Mass,* revised edition. Chicago: Liturgy Training Publications, 2011.

Fagerberg, David W. *On Liturgical Asceticism*. Washington, DC: Catholic University of America Press, 2013.

Faust, Jennifer L. and Donald R. Paulson. "Active Learning in the College Classroom." *Journal on Excellence in College Teaching* 9, no. 2 (1998): 3–24.

Forrest, Tom, CSsR. "Why Should Catholics Evangelize?" In *John Paul II and the New Evangelization*, edited by Ralph Martin and Peter Williamson, 35. Cincinnati, OH: Servant Books, 2006.

Francis. "Address to Participants in the Pilgrimage of Catechists on the Occasion of the Year of Faith and of the International Congress on Catechesis (September 27, 2013)." Vatican.va.

———. *Evangelii Gaudium*. Vatican Translation. Boston: Pauline Books and Media, 2013.

Giussani, Luigi. *The Religious Sense*. Translated by John Zucchi. Montreal: McGill-Queens University Press, 1997.

Greene, Graham. *The End of the Affair*. New York: Penguin Books, 1995.

Hugo, Victor. *Les Misérables*. San Diego, CA: Canterbury Classics, 2012.

John of the Cross. *The Collected Works of Saint John of the Cross*. Translated by Kieran Kavanaugh, OCD, and Otilio Rodriguez, OCD. Washington, DC: Institute of Carmelite Studies, 1991.

John Paul II. *Catechesi Tradendae*. Boston: Pauline Books and Media, 1979.

———. *Christifideles Laici*. Vatican Translation. Boston: Pauline Books and Media, 1988.

———. *Evangelium Vitae*. Vatican Translation. Boston: Pauline Books and Media, 1995.

———. *Familiaris Consortio*. Vatican Translation. Boston: Pauline Books and Media, 1981.

———. *Redemptoris Missio*. Vatican Translation. Boston: Pauline Books and Media, 1991.

Keating, James. "Teaching Out of Our Desire for God." *The Catechetical Review* 2, no. 1 (April 2016): 9–10.

Keimig, William. "Liturgical Catechesis in the RCIA Process." In *Liturgical Catechesis in the 21st Century: A School of Discipleship*, by James C. Pauley, 198–213. Chicago: Liturgy Training Publications, 2017.

Kelly, Francis D. *The Mystery We Proclaim — Second Edition: Catechesis for the Third Millennium*. Huntington, IN: Our Sunday Visitor, 1999.

Lewis, C. S. *Mere Christianity*. London: Collins, 1952.

Marie-Eugene of the Child Jesus, OCD. "The Child's Potential for Contact with God." Translated by Teresa Hawes. *The Sower* 35, no. 3 (July 2014): 32–33.

———. *I Want to See God: A Practical Synthesis of Carmelite Spirituality*. Translated by Sr. M. Verda Clare, CSC. Notre Dame, IN: Fides Publishers, 1953.

———. *Where the Spirit Breathes: Prayer and Action*. Translated by Sr. Mary Thomas Noble, OP. New York: Alba House, 1998.

Marmion, Columba, OSB. *Christ in His Mysteries*. Bethesda, MD: Zaccheus Press, 2008.

———. *Christ the Life of the Soul*. Bethesda, MD: Zaccheus Press, 2005.

Martin, Ralph. "What Is the New Evangelization?" *The Catechetical Review* 1, no. 1 (January 2015): 6–7.

McCormack, Sr. Patricia M., IHM. "Children's Catechesis: Forming a Culture of Prayer within the Home." *The Catechetical Review* 4, no. 4 (October 2018): 30–32.

Morgan, Barbara and Sr. Athanasius Munroe, OP. *Echoing the Mystery: Unlocking the Deposit of Faith in Catechesis*. Ann Arbor, MI: Lumen Ecclesiae Press, 2018.

Mother Teresa. In *The Joy in Loving: A Guide to Daily Living*. Edited by Jaya Chalika and Edward Le Joly. New York: Penguin Books, 1997.

Mouroux, Jean. *From Baptism to the Act of Faith*. Translated by Sister M. Elizabeth, IHM, and Sister M. Johnice, IHM. Boston: Allyn and Bacon,

1964.

O'Malley, Timothy P. *Divine Blessing: Liturgical Formation in the RCIA*. Collegeville, MN: Liturgical Press, 2019.

Paul VI. *Evangelii Nuntiandi*. Boston: Pauline Books and Media, 1976.

Philippe, Jacques. *Time for God*. Strongsville, OH: Scepter Publishers, 2008.

Roan McKeegan, Maura. "Reading with Love: Tips for Sharing Spiritual Books with Children." St. Paul Center (August 14, 2009). https://stpaulcenter .com/reading-with-love-tips-for-sharing-spiritual-books-with-children

de Sales, Francis. *Introduction to the Devout Life*. Translated by John K. Ryan. New York: Doubleday, 1989.

Sarah, Robert Cardinal with Nicolas Diat. *The Power of Silence: Against the Dictatorship of Noise*. Translated by Michael J. Miller. San Francisco: Ignatius Press, 2017.

Second Vatican Council. "Ad Gentes." In *Vatican Council II: The Conciliar and Post Conciliar Documents*. Edited by Austin Flannery. Northport, NY: Costello Publishing Co., 1996.

———. "Lumen Gentium." In *Vatican Council II: The Conciliar and Post Conciliar Documents*. Edited by Austin Flannery. Northport, NY: Costello Publishing Co., 1996.

———. "Sacrosanctum Concilium." In *Vatican Council II: The Conciliar and Post Conciliar Documents*. Edited by Austin Flannery. Northport, NY: Costello Publishing Co., 1996.

Sheed, Frank. *Are We Really Teaching Religion?* New York: Sheed and Ward Inc., 1953.

Siegel, Elizabeth. "Opening the Treasures of the Church: The Catechism in Adult Faith Formation." *The Catechetical Review* 5, no. 4 (October 2019): 34–35.

———. "Part Four: Christian Prayer." In Petroc Willey, Fr. Dominic Scotto, Donald Asci, and Elizabeth Siegel, *A Year with the Catechism: 365 Day Reading Plan*. Huntington, IN: Our Sunday Visitor, 2018.

Sullivan, Jem. *The Beauty of Faith: Using Christian Art to Spread the Good News*. Huntington, IN: Our Sunday Visitor, 2009.

Teresa of Jesus. *The Book of Her Life*. In *The Collected Works of Saint Teresa of Ávila*. Translated by Kieran Kavanaugh, OCD, and Otilio Rodriguez, OCD. Washington, DC: Institute of Carmelite Studies, 1976.

————. *The Interior Castle.* In *The Collected Works of Saint Teresa of Ávila.* Translated by Kieran Kavanaugh, OCD, and Otilio Rodriguez, OCD. Washington, DC: Institute of Carmelite Studies, 1980.

Thérèse of Lisieux. *The Story of a Soul: The Autobiography of Saint Thérèse of Lisieux.* Translated by John Clark, OCD. 3rd ed. Washington, DC: ICS Publications, 1996.

Timmermans, Felix. *The Perfect Joy of Saint Francis.* Translated by L. A. Aspelagh. San Francisco: Ignatius Press, 1998.

Tolkien, J. R. R. *The Two Towers.* New York: Ballantine Books, 1988.

Troisi, Simone and Cristiana Paccini. *Chiara Corbella Petrillo: A Witness to Joy.* Translated by Charlotte J. Fasi. Manchester, NH: Sophia Institute Press, 2015.

United States Conference of Catholic Bishops Committee on Education and Committee on Catechesis. *National Directory for Catechesis.* Washington, DC: USCCB Publishing, 2005.

Weddell, Sherry. *Forming Intentional Disciples: The Path to Knowing and Following Jesus.* Huntington, IN: Our Sunday Visitor, 2012.

Wegemer, Gerard B. *Thomas More: A Portrait of Courage.* Princeton, NJ: Scepter Publishers, 1995.

White, Joseph D. "Children's Catechesis: Five Ways Psychology Can Inform Catechesis." *The Catechetical Review* 3, no. 3 (July 2017): 33–35.

About the Author

Dr. James Pauley is professor of theology and catechetics at Franciscan University of Steubenville, where he has served since 2002. He is author of the book *Liturgical Catechesis in the 21st Century: A School of Discipleship* (Liturgy Training Publications, 2017). In 2014, James was appointed editor of *The Catechetical Review*, Franciscan University's journal dedicated to catechetics and evangelization. James began working as a parish catechetical leader in 1989 and has served professionally in parish, diocesan, and university catechetical formation for more than thirty years. Having received his doctorate in sacred theology from the Liturgical Institute at the University of Saint Mary of the Lake/Mundelein Seminary in 2014, he is a frequent speaker in dioceses and parishes nationwide. James is married to Katrina, and they are blessed with three beautiful daughters.